The Joy of Propaganda

The Joy of Propaganda

The How and Why of Public Relations and Marketing

By Jeff Bradford

ISBN: 979-8-9872879-0-3 (paperback)

First Edition

For Jeanne, who made it possible.

Contents

Writing

How

Why

Public Relations

How

Why

Marketing

How

Why

Management

How

Why

Preface

This little book is a kind of commercial memoir: gleanings from a life of work in words.

This journey in words began a few years after college with the editorship of a small and struggling weekly newspaper where I did most everything but print the paper, including writing the stories, taking the photos, selling ads — even carrying papers to country stores spread around the county (where I also picked up the news). It was literally a hero journey. I lasted a year. It was exhausting even for a twenty-something.

After a few more years in the newspaper business making a four-figure salary, I eventually found my way to the PR industry and have spent most of my professional life working in public relations and advertising agencies — including the last 20 years as head of my own PR firm, the Bradford Group, which, exactly on the company's 20th anniversary, I sold to pursue new adventures in the hometown I left over 40 years ago. Kind of an elderly hero quest. Stay tuned.

During my latter years at the Bradford Group, I did a lot of writing about the PR profession because I finally knew enough to share some of it and I needed to feed the agency blog's insatiable appetite for original content. This book compiles these writings and others, including articles written for *Forbes, Inc, Fast Company* and other publications.

I write about things that engage me every day and have for decades — writing, PR, marketing and management. There are lots of books on these topics, of course. No doubt you'll find ideas here you've heard before (there is nothing new under the sun, of course), but I hope they are presented in a way that allows you to see new truths, or see old truths in new ways that are more likely to lead to action.

Winston Churchill once said, "I like things to happen, and if they don't happen I like to make them happen." This idea of "making things happen" has been the NorthStar of my commercial life. Though I like thinking as much as the next 21st Centurion, I don't believe thinking is enough. It is little more than amusement unless it leads to action. Indeed, in some ways, thinking does not really exist until it manifests itself in physical reality. This pragmatic approach pervades this book. It is full of "how to" articles for making things happen.

But (and perhaps it sets this book apart) it's not all meat and potatoes. "How" is balanced with "why" in an attempt to understand the invisible forces that drive visible results. This search for the power behind things cobbles together widely divergent disciplines — Jungian psychology and marketing theory, or literature and commerce, for example. Hopefully these "why" chapters are entertaining. I am optimistic that a few are even enlightening.

In any case, this is an easy book to peruse, so feel free to concentrate on the "how" chapters and ignore the "why" ones or, if you like, the other way around. Or just dip in and out of the many topics covered. (The most popular chapter, by far, is "Why Writing Ability Is the Most Important Skill in Business — And How to Acquire It.")

My wish is that you'll find here what I found during my long sojourn in the field of propaganda: a good mixture of "how" and "why," with enough "how" to get things done and enough "why" to keep you interested.

Jeff Bradford
January 2023

The Case for Worthless College Majors

There is a lot of talk these days about people who chose a "worthless" college major and are surprised they can't find a job that pays enough to retire their student loans.

I'm one of those people who chose such a major — two of them in fact: English and philosophy. Looking back, it was one of the best decisions of my life. Not only was I able to earn a good living, but I have experienced the joy of lifelong learning and the fulfillment of a career that made the most of my education. It also led to the freedom of starting and owning my own business. And the freedom to sell it and reap its gain.

A liberal arts education helps you understand what makes you happy and provides a roadmap to happiness.
Just add discipline and focus.

Thanks to my worthless majors, I'm a professional propagandist, a vocation I truly enjoy. For this calling there is no better preparation than the study of how we speak and how we think, and how to do both well: English and philosophy.

If you are a literary person, public relations is your dream job. Essentially, you get to write term papers on a variety of topics, dipping into the knowledge and ways of thinking that a liberal arts education affords. Sometimes, you can even make literary references that illiterate people can understand. That is, create helpful jargon. Which is pretty good. It's art.

And people pay me and my associates to do this. Quite well, actually.

And that is the life and business case for the liberal arts. In toto. Here is the journey

1. Follow your bliss
2. Organize
3. Focus
4. Discern

To *follow your bliss* means finding it, of course, by being introspective and aware of what you are thinking and feeling. For me, this process led to art. I'm fascinated by the "artifice" of language, for example — working out the most mellifluent and economic way to communicate, whether in words or paint or sculpture or recipes. That's fun. And I learned this from reading literature, which is not just good writing, but good ideas expressed well.

But, at some point, the young artist learns philosophy, and then it's a new world. Empirical. Guided by reason. ***Organized and objective.*** And wisdom is there, too. For instance, knowing the difference between Platonic and Aristotelian philosophies, and the benefits and deficits of each, helps me to wade through and weigh ideas — whether I'm writing a news release or buying a new copier for our business. Reason is an anchor.

So, thanks to my worthless majors, I know what makes me happy: art. (The reason I majored in English.) And, I know how to navigate the passage, thanks to philosophy. That is, I know where others have trod, the systems they worked out. The marriage of art and philosophy made me an effective propagandist, one who can sniff out the situation, advise on the best course and communicate it elegantly. AKA a public relations expert.

With this artistic and philosophic base, add ego, which drives the self-directed narrowing of interests and perception needed to acquire mastery. *A focus.* This process is not affected by education. Savage people can be very focused and effective. This is discipline and perseverance. It's character.

The first and last stage of life and business is *discernment* — judging which is best. This requires knowledge and self-awareness: reason and art. We end where we started, like a uroboros. The dragon eating his tail, universal symbol of both cycles and unity, which is, itself, aesthetic wisdom.

That is why a liberal arts education is valuable, or can be. It helps you understand what makes you happy and provides a roadmap to happiness. Just add discipline and focus and this liberal arts brew allows one to choose wisest in both business and life.

Now, a word about a word: propaganda. Why would I knowingly use such a vulgar term to describe my profession?

For several reasons, including the word's originally meaning. As I put it in the "About the Editor" section of my personal blog, "The Joy of Propaganda:"

"The word 'propaganda,' which is Latin for 'propagation,' originates with the Roman Catholic church, which established the Congregatio de Propaganda Fide, or "congregation for propagating the faith," in 1622 to handle the Church's mission activities. Thus, propaganda truly began as a joyful enterprise."

I also think it simply sounds much better than "public relations practioneer," the aesthetically catastrophic *nom de plume* bequeathed by PRSA, PR's professional organization.

Being able to make an aesthetic decision — which combines emotional and rational discernment — is the essence of PR.

So, I suppose I prefer "propagandist" to "public relations practioneer" on aesthetic grounds alone. And for a worthless major, that is enough.

- Originally appeared in Forbes

Writing

All effective PR and marketing programs spring from and are guided by effective writing.

First, as this book notes more than once, good writing is simply good thinking made visible. The process we follow when we write well is very similar to the process of thinking clearly. And clear, organized and honest thinking is behind every successful marketing effort, and anything done well, for that matter.

Second, writing is fundamental to PR and marketing. It is the most-used tool in the profession, which could not exist without it. If you are not a proficient writer, you simply do not have the necessary equipment to do the job.

How To Write Like a Gunslinger

I like gunfighters. Quick draw duels on a dusty mining town street are the norm, and they are fun, but my favorite gunslinger scene is in the movie "Open Range" when Kevin Costner simply walks up to the bad guy who is taunting him from the street and shoots him in the forehead from about a foot away. No banter. No swagger. No macho theatrics. No chance of missing. Just getting the job done.

The best kind of writing is like this. It's quick, clear and rivets your attention.

Here's how to write like a gunslinger:

Say it well once

A frequent problem is saying the same thing in a string of sentences. It's like the writer is not really sure he said it correctly the first time, so he adds another sentence, then another, saying it again in a slightly different way. This redundancy wastes the reader's time and tries her patience.

> *Often, a failure to get to the point is a sign the writer really does not know what he is talking about.*

This is especially a problem in business and management books. Often the author has three to four ideas that can be easily communicated in 20 pages. But no one will pay for a 20-page book, so he says it again and again and again for 200 pages. (I find it maddening to read most business books and avoid doing so whenever I can. Hopefully, this is not a typical business book.)

So, take enough time to write it well once. Of course, it will probably take more than one sentence — that is, you may need to use examples to flesh it out a point, or you may need to talk about different aspects of your idea, and that's okay. But don't ever simply restate what you said with no additional information.

Remember, most gunfights are over in one shot.

Get to the point

Like Kevin Costner's direct approach, a good gunfight involves few preliminaries. You draw. You shoot. Somebody dies.

Do the same in your writing. Don't spend paragraphs leading up to your point. Let readers know what you are talking about right off the bat. This allows them to quickly decide if they care to read what you've written, doing them a great courtesy.

Often, a failure to get to the point is a sign the writer really does not know what he is talking about. He hopes that by putting a lot of words on the paper that some of them might say what he is trying to explain. Readers sense this like animals smell fear.

Say what you mean

There is never any question about where a gunfighter stands on an issue. You should be the same in your writing.

I don't mean that you must think only in black-or-white terms, but that you should state clearly what you mean, no matter how complex the issue, without obfuscation. Be specific. General statements communicate very little.

Say something meaningful

Gunfights are worth watching because they are about something important — important enough for the gunfighters to risk their lives.

Similarly in writing. If you remember that writing is about the reader, not the writer, you'll realize that the only thing worse than writing poorly is writing about unimportant things, because it wastes the reader's time, assuming she will read it to begin with.

Now, this does not mean that you should only write about world-changing ideas, or that meaning can't be drawn from apparently insignificant things. But what you write about should certainly be meaningful to *you*, the writer. If it is, and you're honest and talented, you'll be able to communicate this meaning to your reader.

But, if the subject of your writing is not important to you, then you're likely to lapse into the laziness of jargon and cliché, which is deadly to readers.

Be quick

It took Kevin Costner about three seconds, maybe two, to kill the bad guy. And it was powerful theater.

If he had taken longer, if he had talked about how much he hated the bad guy and exactly how he was going to kill him, or if it had taken two or three bullets to kill him, it would have fallen flat.

Say what you mean to say clearly, then stop. Every unneeded word robs your writing of vitally and your reader of precious time. When you think you've finished, read it over and cut at least 10 percent. (As was done with this book.) Make sure every adjective and adverb is essential. Kill every semi-colon that can't defend itself; they are often signposts of redundancy. Be wary of any paragraph more than four sentences long (like this one, which had to prove its worth).

Use as few bullets as possible.

(See chapter "Why Writing Ability Is the Most Important Skill in Business – And How to Acquire It" for more on economy in writing.)

How To Hire Great Writers

Our PR firm is a company of writers. Writing ability is essential to our vocation.

There are other ways than writing to communicate, of course, but proficient writing requires you to organize your thoughts, and to know the rules we depend upon to understand each other and to empathize with others — which makes it the foundation of effective communication.

The only sure way to know if someone can write
is to give them a writing test.

So, how do you find talented writers? Well, you could ask people during a job interview if they have writing skills and if they say, "yes," ask them to describe what skillful writing is and how their writing measures up to this standard. If they can answer these questions coherently, then they may, in fact, be writers. Or they may just be glib interviewees. We've all hired people who were wonderful during the interview but duds on the job.

Or you can do what most companies do who hire writers: ask to see examples of their published work. The problem is you don't really know how much of it is their work. They may have been heavily edited. Or they may have not actually done the work. For example, college instructors today often have their students work in groups to complete projects. As a result, the smartest student does most of the work and everyone else in the group gets equal credit. This bizarre pedagogy not only allows many college students to graduate with little actual knowledge, but makes it nearly impossible for employers to judge the capabilities of job applicants. I can only assume that professors follow this bizarre practice because it reduces the number of papers to grade.

The only sure way to know if someone can write is to give them a writing test. We use such a test as a screener of job applicants. We only look at resumes of those who pass.

How to create a writing test

It's really quite simple: provide job applicants with a page of information and ask them to write a five- to seven-paragraph story using this information. For example, we provide a page with "facts" about a fictious city and convention center. It does not matter what "facts" you provide. What matters is what those completing the test do with them.

How to "grade" a writing test

This is the hard part, because you must be a good writer to know what good writing looks like. But, if you are not, here are some signs of proficient writing:

Lack of redundancy

People who don't know what they want to say usually say it several times. Restating things in different words that adds nothing to the reader's understanding is bad writing. Talented writers say it well once.

Order and flow

The point the writer seeks to make should be clear and the argument to support the point should proceed in a logical fashion, with appropriate transitions between each step. Writers who do not know how to order their thoughts typically throw a bunch of disjointed facts on the page with no attempt to connect them into a coherent story.

Proper sentence structure

Every sentence should have a subject and a verb. For example, "Some boys in the class." is a sentence fragment, as it is missing a verb. "Some boys in the class study quite hard." is a complete sentence.

And every sentence should communicate a single complete thought — not two or three, which is known as a run-on sentence, and is a more common error than sentence fragments. Here is an example of a run-on sentence: "Thanks to everyone who showed up at the meeting, while it was virtual, we did try to make it interesting, and most people seemed to like it."

Uses active voice

Writing in the active voice is typically more powerful than using the passive voice, which tends to sound weaselly. In a passive sentence, the subject is acted on by the verb; in an active one, the subject performs the action stated by the verb. Probably the most used and cowardly passive sentence is "Mistakes were made." An active version of this sentence requires someone to take responsibility: "We made mistakes."

Is concise

"Sorry for the long letter. I didn't have time to write a short one." It is difficult to distill your thoughts down to as few words as possible, but good writers can do it. Poor writers ramble.

Ultimately, creating, administering and grading a writing test just takes experience. After you've read about 50 tests, you'll begin to get a sense of what is good and what is not. The key is to use the same set of facts every time you give the test, as this will allow you to compare how different people work with the same building blocks. Some can build beautiful cathedrals of words. Some can't nail two boards together.

- Originally appeared in Forbes

Buzzwords That Will Doom Your PR and Marketing Resume

Looking for a job in the PR and marketing business? Keep in mind that effective communication is the cornerstone of this industry. If your resume or cover letter is poorly written, it doesn't matter how many impressive internships your resume lists or how many glowing referrals you tack on. You're already dead.

Since the marketing industry is often seen as sexy and fun, it is deluged with resumes. Yours needs to stand out, but not for the wrong reasons, like using any of these killer buzzwords.

Pomposity has its place, such as in satire.
Anywhere else, and the joke is on you.

People person

Describing yourself thusly probably means everything you know about PR and marketing came from watching TV sitcoms, where the PR person is the girl who goes to parties. A friendly, compelling personality can certainly be a plus in this business, but only if it's matched with intelligence and the ability to make stuff happen — traits that do not leap to mind when you hear "people person."

Literally

Nine out of 10 times you mean "figuratively" — that is, the opposite of "literally." And if your writing literally communicates the opposite of what you mean, then you literally cannot communicate — and communication is literally essential in PR and marketing.

Comprise

Because you probably mean "compose," and if you don't know what words mean, it's unlikely you're much of communicator. I assume college communications departments are largely composed of professors who are members of a fan-club comprising lovers of the word "comprise," because I see it a lot of it these days. (Parts compose the whole. The whole comprises the parts.) I assume people think it's a more sophisticated way of saying "compose." It's not.

"It's" when you mean "its," and vice versa

The quickest way to identify a lack of writing talent is seeing confusion about "it's" (a contraction for "it is") and "its" (the possessive of "it.") When we find this, we usually assume that the college degree is fake — or it took six years to obtain, which is about the same thing.

Emoticons

So, you couldn't come up with a word to describe your feelings? And you're a great communicator?

Unique

"Unique" literally means "one of a kind," not "really cool." So, if you tell me you've done something "unique," chances are that you actually haven't — and I start wondering what else you're lying about in your resume.

Awesome

Thanks to extreme overuse, this word means nothing — or everything. Either way, it communicates no information, other than the paucity of your vocabulary (and, by extension, your lack of interest in original thinking).

Impact

This word encapsulates all that is awful about the way 21st Century humans relate to each other. We don't affect something, we impact it. And the effect we have is an impact. All of this smashing and mashing sounds painful. It's the vocabulary of pretentious thugs.

Utilize

What is the difference between "use" and "utilize?" One word is used by people who want to communicate clearly. The other is utilized by those who think intelligence is measured by the number of syllables in your words. It ain't. Pomposity has its place, such as in satire. Anywhere else, and the joke is on you.

Non-Anglo-Saxon words

English is an amalgamation of words from many languages, but especially Anglo-Saxon (spoken by the Germanic tribes who invaded England when the Romans left), Norman French (thanks to the Norman Invasion in 1066) and Latin (the language of the Church). So, in many cases, we have three ways of saying the same thing, such as "ask" (Anglo-Saxon), "question" (Norman French) and "interrogate (Latin), or "goodness," "virtue" and "probity," or "rise," "mount" and "ascend." Since good writing is clear writing, it's often wise to rely on the foundation of our language, Anglo-Saxon words.

This is not a hard-and-fast rule, of course. Due to the shades of meaning words have acquired over the millennia, there can be many reasons why "virtue" or even "probity" is a better choice than "goodness" in a particular situation — but it should be a conscious choice. Using a $10 word when a nickel one will work doesn't impress anybody. In fact, just the opposite. Like wearing a tuxedo to a pig roast, you just look foolish.

Business jargon

Because at the end of the day it's never a best practice, and certainly not a win-win on a go-forward basis, to try to leverage your skill set and hit all the touchpoints in a synergistic fashion with an inane vocabulary that proves you can't think outside the box.

How To Write an Obituary

If you are a public relations executive of a certain age, you'll write obituaries. You're simply the most qualified person to handle this delicate and important assignment.

The heads of PR agencies and leaders of corporate PR departments get to know their clients or bosses very well because PR tends to be personal and focused on the big picture, as well as dealing with big problems. You're also the person writing executives' speeches and dinner remarks, as well as writing their quotes for press releases, bylined columns and so forth. So, you've learned their voice, as well as what they hold dear and what they don't.

> *If you are called upon to write a friend's obituary,*
> *I think you will find it to be*
> *one of the easiest and most satisfying things you'll ever do.*

Obituaries are a different kind of writing. You don't churn them out every day. I've written two in my career. Here are the lessons I learned:

First, ask the family if they prefer "died" or "passed away." Passed away is the gentlest, of course, and usual term if there is no direction from the family. For some people — those who faced life head-on, who were frank and honest — "passed away" is a white lie they didn't need. Anyway, decide this first.

In the first paragraph, sum up the person's life in a way that tells a story. Don't just list jobs and charities — use them to weave a narrative of the deceased's life. Find a theme, the message of the obituary. For example, "John Smith, architect, saw things others didn't and then did something about it. The result ranged from designing daring buildings to volunteering at his church's homeless shelter."

Write the second paragraph last because here is where you want some statement of who the person was and the values they lived by. These larger themes may not be evident before you finish the obit.

Skip to the third paragraph and tell the story of their life through a recitation of their resume, but not just a listing of companies and titles and charities. You're telling this person's biography – telling it, not writing it, so you begin where you would in telling a story. For example, "When he graduated college in 1970, he left for New York to experience the energy and ideas of the world, taking a junior position at Standfeld & Stanley and playing a significant role in the design of several apartment buildings in Brooklyn."

Then take it back to the beginning. Talk about their birthplace, siblings and early memories, jobs, adventures, and perhaps an early hero story during the days when they first took on the world. Did your friend really set up a lemonade stand at 9 years old? That's a hero story. Starting any business before age 25 is heroic. If possible – if there is really information to work with – celebrate this time of the deceased's life, this energy. It breathes life into this death-focused piece of writing.

End by listing survivors, and then the date, time and place of the funeral. And think about appending to the obituary a collection of quotations about the deceased from people who knew them well. As those of us who have written our share of press releases know, quotes are where you get to talk about the benefits, not just the features. They are how you inject emotion. They also give the reader a real feel for who the person was, as seen from many different perspectives of people who loved them.

If you are called upon to write a friend's obituary, I think you will find it to be one of the easiest and most satisfying things you'll ever do. Easy, because you really must be a good friend of the deceased's to be asked to write the obituary – so you already know a lot of the information you need to write the obit. And what you don't know you can easily find by talking with other friends. Satisfying, because writing an obituary, and doing a respectable job of it, is not only an important service for the family, but also a gift to your friend. And a good memory of them you'll always have.

- *Originally appeared in Forbes*

Why Writing Ability Is the Most Important Skill in Business — And How to Acquire It

Business is fundamentally about convincing people to do things — such as buying your product, giving you a good online review, attending events and other activities — and you can't make these things happen if you can't communicate well.

Communication takes many forms, such as video, speaking, phone calls, texting, email, signage, advertising, blogging, publicity and others. However, doing any of these well requires writing skills.

> *You can't make things happen*
> *if you can't communicate well.*

Why? Because, as we have said before, good writing is fundamentally good thinking. Writing forces you to organize your thoughts, which makes it more likely you'll be understood.

Of course, proficient writing is more than logic in action. It also must touch the reader, listener or viewer emotionally. Otherwise, it won't connect. It won't lead to the behavior you are seeking to create.

What makes a good writer? I suggest it is these things:

Clear thinking

It is impossible to write well without thinking clearly. You must understand what you want to say and be able to explain it. And I'm not talking about intelligence. A dull person can write better than a brilliant one if she clearly understands what she wants to communicate and sticks to it without wandering off into irrelevancies. In fact, smart people are sometimes poor writers because their need to show off can muddy the message. (See "Economy" below.)

Knowing the rules

The best writers regularly break the rules of grammar, but only after they've learned them to the point where they are second nature. It is

14

like the difference between a masterful and hack painter of abstract art: the master first learned how to paint representational art. This firm foundation gives his abstract work a balance and harmony that the hack's will never possess. Picasso said he had to first learn to paint like Raphael before he could paint like a child.

To learn the rules of writing, read *Elements of Style* by Strunk & White. The entire book is available for free online at www.bartleby.com/141.

Good reading habits

Simply knowing how to spell and the rules of grammar does not make you a writer. You must read talented writers to know what skillful writing looks like. And read a variety of writers, so it's less likely you'll parrot someone's style. Reading widely will also fill your brain with information you can use in your writing. So read outstanding literature, of course, but also read about history, biography, science, politics, art, technology and more.

Curiosity

Being curious leads you to read widely and also to carefully observe the world around you, both the animate and inanimate worlds, and to ask questions and seek out people who know things you don't know. Be a lifelong learner and you will continually grow the cognitive and emotional capacity you need to be a capable writer — because you'll learn what moves people to act.

Empathy

As the saying goes, no one cares how much you know until they know how much you care. A lack of empathy for the reader is to blame for most bad writing. It leads to pompous drivel. To be an effective writer you must get outside of yourself and get inside the heads and hearts of others. This will allow you to do two important things: One, say something interesting, because you are able to juxtapose the thoughts of others with your own thoughts — and putting together things in novel ways is the foundation of creativity. Two, you're able to tap into the emotional intelligence that fuels expert writing.

Economy

It takes effort to be succinct, but your reader will appreciate it. Never use three words when one will do. Don't say the same thing twice in a different way. Don't write a preamble before getting to your point.

Avoid adjectives and adverbs. Use more precise nouns or verbs instead. Rather than saying someone cheerfully and quickly accomplished a task, say he accomplished it with alacrity. Don't say someone lightly knocked on the door. Say she tapped on the door.

Unless there is a reason not to, stick to simple Anglo-Saxon words and eschew the Latin and Norman French words that have crept into English. *(See chapter "Buzzwords That Will Doom Your PR and Marketing Resume" for more about the languages that contributed most to modern English.)*

And when you've said what you want to say, stop. Read Hemingway — especially his early books — for examples of economical writing at its best. *(See chapter "Why Literature Matters" for more on Hemingway.)*

Lack of jargon

Jargon is a formulaic way of stating pre-chewed ideas. It's used by people who can't digest original concepts. It makes you look stupid. It annoys people. It is cheap substitute for thinking. It is ugly. Avoid it at all costs. *(See chapter "Why Business Jargon Steals Your Soul.)*

The best way to learn to write well is to write often. Write when you don't feel like it. Write when you think you have nothing to say. Write under a pressing deadline. Write in different formats and learn how to adapt your style to each. Practice, practice, practice. Eventually, writing will come as naturally as speaking — and your speaking will probably become more precise, with fewer "you know" and "like" and "um" and other filler words.

- Originally appeared in Forbes

Why Business Jargon Steals Your Soul

I detest jargon at a visceral level. I not only *understand* how much jargon sabotages our communication, but I *feel* how ugly it is, how it stultifies the soul. It does not deserve to live.

Why do I loathe jargon so? Let me count the ways...

People can't understand you

By definition, and at its best, jargon is specialized language used to communicate quickly and accurately among a group of people who have something in common, such as an occupation, a hobby or a religion. For example, among Catholics, "consubstantial" is a useful piece of jargon, for it quickly and completely (thus elegantly) communicates a quite complex, even mystical formulation of the Christian Trinity. One word takes the place of thousands, but only because those in the group have invested their time in learning about the ideas it communicates. Within the group, it is efficient — the highest compliment for any communication.

> *Often, jargon creeps into our language like curse words*
> *— it's just something we pick up by being around the wrong people.*

However, throw around "consubstantial" in casual conversation and you'll get blank stares. It means nothing to those who aren't in the club. The same applies to business jargon, whether it be industry specific or — the worst — general management jargon. People simply will not understand what you are saying. And they will stop listening — if they ever started, which is doubtful.

You don't understand yourself

Even worse, you probably don't fully understand the jargon you use. Does anyone really know what "boil the ocean" means? Or "ideation?" Or, my favorite, "solutioneering?"

Often, jargon creeps into our language like curse words — it's just something we pick up by being around the wrong people. In fact, watching someone use jargon in a business meeting or sales pitch is like watching a child curse for the first time. He doesn't really know what he is saying, but he's seen grown-ups say it, and it sounds powerful.

The next time someone says he wants to "solutioneer" a problem, ask him what he really means. He probably won't have the slightest idea. But it sure sounds a lot more sophisticated than "solving" a problem. So, it must be better. Right?

You don't think

Often, jargon is a substitute for thinking — or, at least, original thinking. Business jargon speed dials thoughts that have been thought many times before and have lost their luster.

For example, the first person who used the term "best practices" was probably describing his discovery — i.e., an original thought — that you could improve a process by closely watching what talented people do. The first genius who came up with the concept of "scalability" communicated a clear and exact concept because he had spent a lot of time studying how small enterprises become large ones.

These terms have now become shopworn tools that lazy people substitute for thinking. Have a problem? No problem, we'll just survey best practices and develop synergistic, robust and actionable steps that we'll run up the flagpole for buy-in from all stakeholders. Then, we'll take it offline to find the secret sauce that will enhance our scalability. No thinking required. The jargon does it for you. (Until you actually have to do something. Not just talk about it.)

It's for followers, not leaders

Because jargon is largely about pre-chewed ideas, it's used by people who can't digest original concepts. Leaders come up with the ideas that eventually get transformed into jargon when the ideas have lost their vitality.

So, if you want to be a leader, speak like one. Describe your thoughts accurately with precise language so that people have a clear idea of what you have in mind. If you speak, write and think this way you will find it impossible to use business jargon, which is almost exclusively about communicating fuzzy concepts that will get a mediocre person through a meeting but lead nowhere.

It is simply ugly

I am viscerally disgusted by jargon on aesthetic grounds. As a writer, I think language is naturally beautiful. I like the way it sounds. I like the way it facilitates the flow of ideas and emotions. I like the way it makes us human.

Jargon is a chancre on this beauty, primarily because it reeks of cheap pretentions. Why would someone say "utilize" instead of the good old Anglo-Saxon "use" if not because they think a three-syllable word sounds more refined that a one-syllable one? However, unless you have a good reason for "utilizing" instead of "using" (and such reasons do exist), you are pretending to a sophistication you do not possess, and are, thus, a fool. You are truly, as the jargon goes, putting lipstick on a pig.

Like many evil practices, jargon promises easy access to wisdom, sophistication and privilege (at least the appearance of such). In fact, it leads to weakness of mind and spirit and ultimately, ignominy — or worse, irrelevance. If you wish to think clearly and lead confidently, avoid the siren song of jargon.

- Originally appeared in Forbes

Why Technology Needs English Majors

I am a student of English and philosophy who spends a substantial portion of his reading time with books about modern physics. One of my plans for retirement is to go back to school to learn the mathematics necessary to truly understand the physics books I am reading.

We breathe the myths of our culture
into the machines of our age
to give them meaning and vitality.

We live in a world shaped by the hard sciences, rewarding those who can shape matter to their bidding. It is largely a positivist world, where all that exists is energy and matter (not spirit) and all that matters is how, not why.

What is an English major to do?

We are to make sense of it. Apple understands this. It doesn't sell technology. It sells possibilities, novelty, wonder, discovery, mastery, joy. That's why Apple stores are always packed, and why stores that emphasize only the technology die. (Remember CompUSA? Circuit City?)

And that's what smart public relations counselors and marketers do. We breathe the myths of our culture into the machines of our age to give them meaning and vitality. Creating this emotional connection may be as important as creating the technology, because it creates desire for the technology.

At the other end of this poetical/practical spectrum lies my fascination with the physics behind our technology. The unseen and probably unseeable forces that make the iPhone work are as mystical as the myths used to sell the iPhone. Physics' latest theory postulates that that there are 11 dimensions and that we can only experience four of them because the other seven are "rolled up." And string theory says that vibrating strings of energy are all that exist. Just like Einstein said, energy equals matter. This is mystical.

I understand, or at least understand the language of, the *mythical* end of the spectrum. That's what literature, art and religion are about, which I've spent a lifetime studying. I am by no means an expert in these areas, but I understand the code well enough to "get" it — unlike my situation on the *mystical* end, where my unfamiliarity with mathematics prevents me from truly understanding what the priests of physics are saying.

So, I hope to learn their code and close the circle that begins in mystery, proceeds through matter and ends in mythology, only to begin again in mystery. The parts of this circle that you can't see — mystery and mythology — create and make sense of the matter you can see. The invisible, which includes the mystery of marketing, is essential. The visible, the actual technology, is ephemeral.

And that's why there will always be a place for English majors. Because we tell the stories that people are really buying when they buy a smart phone.

Public Relations

Public relations may be the most fulfilling and most frustrating occupation. Fulfilling because it is fun to make things happen and nothing is better at generating a response than PR. Frustrating because the core of PR – publicity – is not entirely under the control of the public relations consultant: she must convince someone else to transmit her message. And not just anybody, but a journalist, someone trained to be skeptical.

But, as the "Father of PR," Edward Bernays, often pointed out, the field of public relations encompasses much more than publicity. Indeed, it is about how to relate to the public, in general, and therefore makes use of many different tools, including advertising, social media, content marketing, events, word-of-mouth and the many other ways we have devised to persuade one another.

This chapter will explore many facets of public relations with two goals in mind: 1) To help you understand how to use PR tactics to accomplish something and 2) to transmit some of the mystery of the profession that makes it so fascinating.

How To Think Like a Journalist

Effective public relations professionals have many talents. They are excellent writers. They know how to interview people to uncover interesting information. They are doggedly determined. They are naturally curious and voracious readers across a wide variety of subjects.

And, most importantly for generating publicity — the heart of PR — they know how to think like a journalist. Here's how they do it:

Focus on the new

"News" is about what is new. Thinking like a journalist means being constantly on the lookout for things that have not happened before. This is where being naturally curious and a voracious reader comes in handy, because you can't know what's new unless you know what's happened before.

> *Journalists don't care what you think or speculate.*
> *They care what you know and can prove.*

You should know everything there is to know about your industry, and then a little about everything else, so you can know when your company has done something never done before, inside or outside your industry. This kind of deep and wide knowledge also makes you a valuable resource to journalists. Combine this with trust — earned by providing honest and valuable information in the past — and a journalist will rely on you to tell them what's new in your industry.

Look for the superlative

A corollary of "the new" is the superlative — something unique because it has taken some aspect of itself to the extreme. For example, it might be the fastest, the slowest, the largest, the smallest, the cheapest, the most expensive, the loudest, the quietest, the youngest, the oldest, the cleanest, the filthiest, the safest, the most dangerous and so on. The list of superlatives is virtually endless. So, if you can't be "firstest" (i.e., new), then find a way to be the "mostest."

Deal in facts and stats, not opinions

In general, journalists don't care what you think or speculate. They care what you know and can prove. So, be prepared to share hard, verifiable facts with journalists.

The only journalists who care about opinions are those who cover politics but, even then, they only care about the opinions of people who have the authority to act on them — making them facts — or whose opinions have been borne out by facts in the past.

Stand out from the crowd

Journalists can gather information from many people in your industry, including your competitors — so offer something different. If everyone in your industry shares the same facts, then provide a distinct perspective on these facts, and show why your perspective matters — how it affects what people think of your industry, or how it allows you to better serve your customers, or be kinder to the environment, for example.

Be accessible

The most successful journalists ensure news can find them. They answer the phone, respond to Tweets, work all hours and, in general, do whatever it takes to open themselves to opportunity. You should follow their lead and be accessible to journalists. Return their phone calls and emails quickly — certainly before their deadline — and when you don't know the answer to one of their questions, find it and get back to them quickly.

Be honest

Good journalists are among the most honest people on the planet. They must be willing to follow a story wherever it leads, even if it contradicts what they believe. And they must be extremely trustworthy with their contacts, because if they are not, no one will talk with them, and they will be cut off from their most valuable resource — people who know what journalists don't know and are willing to share it with them. You need to be just as honest. Always tell journalists the truth about what you know and don't pretend to know what you don't.

This doesn't mean you must tell journalists everything you know — you should never divulge trade secrets or proprietary information, for example, even "off the record" — but never lie. The first time you're caught in a lie is the last time a journalist will talk with you.

Be quotable

I once had a client who was prone to making somewhat audacious statements, like openly calling out people in power or pointing out how the current situation favors one group over another or using exaggeration to make a point. This made him very quotable because journalists are looking for people who say bold things. It makes readers sit up and take notice.

Most people, particularly businesspeople, tend to use bland language so not to offend anyone who might help them — like a prospective customer — or hurt them — like a government official who has regulatory power over their industry. This is prudent, of course, but it is unlikely to get a journalist's attention. So, if you can afford it, be bold!

Basically, thinking like a journalist means to be an alert and interested person who is confident of what she knows and is willing to share what's not confidential. Which is actually a pretty good way to live your life anyway, but has the advantage of making it more likely that the news media will help you raise awareness of your business.

- Originally appeared in Forbes

How To Get Journalists' Attention

Journalists are bombarded with hundreds of messages a day. It's not easy to get their attention. Here are a few tips for breaking through the clutter in pitching news stories:

Remember it's sales

If you are a business owner, you already know how to sell, or you wouldn't be in business. Pitching a story is like pitching anything else. Most of the sales rules and tips you already know apply. But don't try to *sell* journalists your product, help them *solve* their problem by providing access to people who have a story to tell that will interest the journalist's readers — or, more importantly, will interest her editors.

> *Pitching a story is like pitching anything else.*
> *Most of the sales rules and tips you already know apply.*

Know the definition of news

News is something out of the ordinary, such as being the first, only, newest, biggest, smallest, etc. For example, being the first in your industry to have an unlimited vacation policy might be news. Being second is not, unless your policy is out of the ordinary, like applying only to Caribbean vacations.

Never pitch a story that is not genuinely newsworthy. Otherwise, you'll develop a reputation for pitching junk, and you'll be ignored when you have real news to share.

Create news

Hold an event, announce a new product, start a new division, carry a new line. Even better: do something no one else has done before — or hasn't done in a long time or done in the same way. The key is to DO something, especially something out of the ordinary.

You can also leverage existing news by localizing a national story, in which you show how a big national story is playing out in your locality. Or be the newest, best or weirdest example of a national story.

Treat journalists like people

Beware of the "60 Minutes Syndrome," in which you assume that "gotcha" journalism is the norm. It's not, especially with writers who cover business. Follow the Golden Rule and treat reporters how you like to be treated. Be friendly and recognize that they are as busy as you are. Journalists make great friends if you like smart, funny, honest, perceptive people.

Know whom you are sending your news to

Always send your information to a specific person, not just "editor" or "news director." Your pitch is more likely to get attention from a reporter who writes about a topic in which you have expertise than it is from an anonymous editor who gets a hundred pitches a day. Call to make sure you have the right person; don't blindly trust information you find on the internet.

It's also helpful to get to know journalists before you need them. This begins by being in the conversation. For example, demonstrate you are knowledgeable about a topic a reporter covers by commenting on their Twitter feeds. If they are local, invite them to lunch to get to know them better.

Give journalists news that is not about your company

We all want to brag about our companies, but you should also provide news about your entire industry, as well. If you become a source for unbiased, "inside" information about your industry, journalists are more likely to accept your calls when you have news to share about your company.

If you can't get a journalist what they need, find a way for someone else to get it for them

NEVER let down a journalist when they call you — if you want them to keep calling. If you don't have the information they need, find someone who does, *even if that person is a competitor.*

ALWAYS follow up

Simply emailing a press release is never enough. Make sure you follow up by email as well as phone to make sure the reporter got the release, to find out if she is interested, to answer any questions or to set up an interview with the right person at your company.

- Originally appeared in Forbes

How To Be a Thought Leader

Being known as a thought leader has the potential to draw business to you because people see you as having answers to their problems.

The best examples of thought leaders are such modern-day Olympians as Jim Collins, Malcolm Gladwell, Richard Branson, Jeff Bezos and Warren Buffet — the kind of people whom normal mortals believe can see things they don't see, because, in fact, they often can.

> *You don't need to be a best-selling author or*
> *own a multi-billion-dollar enterprise to*
> *reap (some of) the benefits of thought leadership.*

You don't need to be a best-selling author or own a multi-billion-dollar enterprise to reap (some of) the benefits of thought leadership, but you must have four things, which everyone listed above has:

1. **Knowledge and Expertise**: You must know more about and be better at something than others in your field.

2. **Significant Experience**: You must be able to back up your claims to expertise with real-world experience.

3. **Cutting Edge Thinking**: You must be able to generate and effectively communicate innovative ideas — not just comment on what is already known

4. **Time and Effort**: You must be willing to commit considerable time to this project.

How do you know if you are a thought leader? You'll know when someone else says you are — someone with the credentials to be taken seriously. You cannot declare yourself to be a thought leader.

And how do you get people to declare you a thought leader? You begin by getting published by reputable publishers. In increasing order of difficultly of getting their attention, and the value of that attention, the types of publishers that matter are:

1. Blog
2. Podcast
3. Trade Publication
4. Local Magazine/Newspaper
5. Local Online News Site
6. Local TV/Radio
7. Self-Published Book (*like this one*)
8. Vanity Book Publisher
9. National Online News Site
10. National Magazine/Newspaper
11. National TV/Radio
12. Traditional Book Publisher

How do you get published? By having the necessary:

1. Knowledge
2. Experience
3. Innovative thinking
4. Time and effort to let the world know you possess these things
5. Understanding of the tactics needed to attract the attention of a publisher

Most people who have a chance of being a thought leader have acquired #1, #2 and #4. If you don't, go get them and come back in 10 years or so. This chapter is about #3 and #5 — becoming an innovative thinker and attracting the attention of a publisher.

How do you become an innovative thinker? The process begins by reading, a lot. My suggestion is at least two books a month, the *New York Times* and *Wall Street Journal* every day, three to five blogs of thought leaders you admire and relevant trade publications. And read widely outside your field. Read about many things that interest you — which will result in cross-fertilization from whence innovative ideas spring.

You should also practice thinking up new ideas. Write down random ideas that pop into your head. Get outside your usual networks to meet and engage with people who think differently than you. Keep a journal and write in it every day. When you begin putting your thoughts on paper, more will come. Once you get the machinery going, you will automatically begin to see connections you could not see before. (The book *Become An Idea Machine* by Claudia Altucher provides daily exercises for creating new ideas.)

And practice the formula followed by most creative people who seek to solve a problem: Ingest lots of information. Let it incubate. Then brainstorm ideas without censor, cull through the ideas you develop, pick out the best ones and refine them.

Once you have your brain in high gear churning out innovative ideas, it's time to attract a publisher. You can begin by publishing in your blog, posting at least weekly

Then, attract the attention of other industry experts. Create and publish a list of these experts on your blog. Write blog posts that include them — quote them, talk about their strategies, praise their successes, relate your journey to theirs. Share these posts on social media. Follow the experts' social media feeds and interact with them by liking, sharing and commenting on their posts.

Sooner or later, they'll notice — invite them to guest post on your blog and offer to guest post on theirs. This is an excellent way to increase traffic to your blog, because the guest blogger will link to your blog — thereby lending the authority of his site to yours. Plus, the guest blogger is likely to share his posts on your blog via his social media channels.

Then, use your blog posts as the starting point to pitch bylined articles to trade news media. Use that success to pitch stories to national media. Then, use that notoriety to seek speaking engagements. Begin local and small, such as speaking to small civic clubs, who are always looking for speakers. Then move to regional, then national conferences, seminars and trade shows — always using your present experience as proof of your ability to perform at the next level. Videotape your speaking engagements, post them on YouTube and use them as your video resume to book more impressive speaking engagements.

One day, three to five years into this process, you'll read in a magazine or on a blog or hear on a video that you're a "thought leader." And you'll know you've made it. And you'll begin reaping the benefits of being a thought leader in terms of more leads for your business.

Or, maybe, you'll discover that you like being a thought leader better than anything you've done before, so you increase your speaking fee to provide a comfortable living and spend the rest of your days sharing your thoughts with people who believe you see things they can't — because, sometimes, you can.

- Originally appeared in Forbes

How To Prepare for and Handle a Media Crisis

For business owners, ranking right up there with public speaking and snakes, is the fear of a media crisis, a situation that usually involves allegations your company has egregiously violated the public's trust.

The good news is that it is really hard to mess up badly and publicly enough to draw the ire of the media — especially for private companies under $100 million in revenue, which I'm guessing account for the vast majority of business owners reading this book. You have a little more to worry about if you run a public company, especially in an industry like tobacco, alcohol, fossil fuels or prison management, but a true media crisis is rare.

Crisis management is NOT about killing a negative story, which, really, can't be done.

The unwelcome news is that if you do something stupid or negligent enough to draw the attention of the news media, there WILL be a story.

Crisis management is NOT about killing a negative story which, really, can't be done — no matter who you are. Crisis management IS about keeping the story to one news cycle, preventing a week-long, month-long or year-long saga of pain and suffering.

That is, there WILL be pain and suffering. But, if you can keep your bad news to a one-day story, your company will likely recover just fine and your life will not, in fact, be ruined.

Here is how to create and execute a plan to keep a media crisis to one day:

- *Decide and write down, in advance, how information will flow during a crisis and who will be involved in this flow.* This document should do two things:

    o Tell employees what to do and who to contact if they become aware that a crisis is imminent or has emerged.

These instructions to employees are usually as simple as: Call this person and tell them what you heard, saw or know, and don't talk to the media until we talk with you.

o   Designate who is on the crisis management team, how information flows within this team, who is responsible for which duties and who the spokespersons are.

- *Brainstorm possible crisis scenarios in advance,* then develop basic message points and recommended actions for each scenario.

o   For example, if the scenario is that the company's customer database is hacked, the message might be: 1) We have learned of a breach affecting X number of customers. 2) We are notifying each customer who may have been affected and rectifying any problems with their account this hack may have caused, 3) As a precaution, we are providing all customers with free identity protection services for the next year. 4) We are working closely with law enforcement to identify and bring the perpetrator to justice. This is the recommended message outline. Recommended actions might include sending a letter to all customers to explain what happened, how it affects them and how to take advantage of the free identity protection service.

Having these two documents in place in advance greatly increases your chances of successfully weathering a media crisis, because it prevents message confusion and assures an organized response – as long as the plan is followed, of course.

Key points to keep in mind during a media crisis are:

- *Remember your goal is to limit news coverage to one day's cycle, not to prevent news coverage.* Focus on getting it over with, not avoiding it. Respond quickly and clearly to media requests – do not hide, do not lie, don't try to cover up.

- *Don't respond before you are fully prepared.* First, gather as much information as you can about the issue so that you are fully informed. Second, develop a narrative that clearly explains what happened and what you are doing about it, then organize this narrative into four to five talking points that will anchor all interaction with the media. Third, brainstorm possible media questions and your answers and, if possible, role play an interview session with someone on your team posing as a reporter. Fourth, prepare a written statement that presents this narrative and talking points. In some cases, particularly for relatively mild crises, providing a written statement to the news media suffices to answer their most pressing questions, one story is produced by all media involved and you're done.

- *Return all media calls the same day you get them, before the reporter's deadline.* Say the same thing to everyone, all based on the approved talking points. If you get a question you can't answer, tell the reporter you will get back to them, then find out the answer and get back to them before their deadline. Never leave a reporter hanging, because the story will be go on without you, and it will usually be worse than if you had returned the call.

That is the basic one-two-three punch of media crisis management: 1) Prepare in advance to assure things move smoothly during a challenging time. 2) If a crisis occurs, first spend some time to gather information and prepare an honest and compelling narrative about what happened and what you are doing to fix it. 3) Engage with the media, don't hide, and say the same thing to everyone.

Crisis Management in Action

T.S. Eliot said that April is the cruelest month, and that was certainly the case one April when several clients called on us to help them deal with media crises. We were able to avert a full-scale, reputation-destroying result in every case.

First, we benefited from a trusting relationship with our clients. When bombs are flying is no time to begin building trust — it must already be there. We had earned it in advance by demonstrating we know what we are doing. Every successful media placement, well-written blog post and effective social media campaign we executed made this point. Having the client's trust in a media crisis allows us to move quickly, which is essential.

> *If you are caught in a lie or a cover-up,*
> *then everything else you say will be dismissed,*
> *or discounted at the least.*

Trust also applies to our relationships with journalists. Because we have proven to them that we always tell the truth and act in good faith, they are more likely to work with us during a crisis. They won't roll over and play dead or avoid reporting on the story, but neither are they likely to play "gotcha" journalism and come to the story with pre-conceived notions about the client's guilt.

Second, we followed Rule One of crisis management: Get everything out there the first day. We anticipated what questions we'd likely get from the media, quickly crafted appropriate responses and quickly responded to all media inquiries. The goal is to make it a one-day story by getting out all information immediately so that reporters have no legitimate reason to follow up the next day.

Third, we decided what our talking points were and stuck with them. Talking points are not an answer to every question, but they are the basis for answering every question, because they frame every answer within an overall narrative. If you establish what the narrative is, you have a better chance of controlling it.

Fourth, we always told the truth. Telling the truth is essential in any public relations effort, but it especially important during a crisis. If you are caught in a lie or a cover-up, then everything else you say will be dismissed, or discounted at the least.

Fifth, we gave the crisis our total attention. Crisis management is not something you can do part time. It must be all you do, at least for the first day.

PR ROI

In terms of attracting attention, creating awareness and generating authentic buzz, public relations is the most effective arrow a marketer has in his quiver. Why? Believability.

Unlike paid, owned and shared media (ads, blogs and social media) — in which the messenger has complete control of the message and how it is delivered — control in earned media (public relations) lies with others, such as the reporter writing the story and the editor deciding when and where (or if) it will be published.

That's the wonderful thing about PR: It just works.
The challenge is proving it.

It is exactly this lack of control that makes publicity more believable, and thus more effective, than other marketing tactics. While a generous portion of the news you read, especially business news, is the result of good work by a PR professional, the average reader does not know this. To most people, all news is the same and, to the degree that they trust the news outlet, important and true. Even if a reader, viewer or listener of a story were to know that it sprang from the efforts of a PR pro, they know that it still had to pass through the filter of a reporter and editor before it got to them, and is, therefore, likely to be important and true.

It's unlikely for that reader to have the same feeling and trust in an advertisement. This logic is why puffery can serve as an adequate legal defense for advertisers claiming to sell "the best that money can buy." As long as someone believes such statements to be true (like the advertiser who made them), these pronouncements of corporate optimism cannot be proven false — unlike false advertising, which is knowingly making an incorrect claim about something that is a provable, objective fact.

Not all ads use puffery, of course, but it is common enough that most reasonable people take with a grain of salt anything they learn from an ad. (For an idea of how prevalent puffery is, think about the 1990 movie "Crazy People," in which the only people who create ads that tell the unvarnished truth are patients in an insane asylum.)

That's the wonderful thing about PR: It just works. The challenge is proving it. Again, it's all about control. You can count clicks on a banner ad, the number of coupons redeemed and other methods advertisers use to measure their work's impact. Yet, there is no way to track the number of people who read a news story your PR firm generated, much less the number who bought something because they read that story. Of course, you could ask purchasers how they found out about you, but their answer might not be so helpful, such as, "Well, I don't know. I saw something about it somewhere."

All hope is not lost. We found a way to put provide an ROI for PR by placing, in online news outlets, bylined columns with an embedded link to the company's website. Because a bylined column is generally published with little to no editing, you can control the content. However, because it is published in an independent news outlet, the reader also sees the content as important and true because it passed through an editorial filter. That is, someone at the news site had to believe that the content was worthwhile.

These bylined online columns are outliers — combining the believability of publicity with the control and measurability of advertising. (Although it is not an exact measurement, because people can still read the column and buy the product without clicking on the website link in the column. And editors can always delete the links in your copy.)

Even with this limitation, the results of our efforts to publish bylined columns with links to the client's website were astounding. In just one year, we saw a 200% growth in number of customer partnerships and a 57% increase in website visits. And users who came to the website from publicity placements instead of from an internet search were stronger prospects. They looked at 32% more pages per session, stayed twice as long on the site and had a low 39% bounce rate.

Startup PR Kit

Though a PR campaign is often exactly what they need to raise their profile and revenues, startup companies and other smaller ventures often can't afford a PR firm. So, it's DIY time. Though results will not be as spectacular or as rapid as would be generated by professionals, startup founders can bootstrap their way to PR success. Here are a few tips:

Learn which journalists cover your industry and be helpful to them

Search for news about your industry and create a list of journalists who author the stories you find. Learn about these journalists. Set up online alerts for their names and read the stories that pop up. If the media outlets in which the stories you find allow comments, make comments that demonstrate your expertise in the subject and, if applicable, link back to the page on your site that proves your

Is doing your own PR a lot of work? Yes.
Is it worth it? Yes.

credibility. Find the journalists' Twitter feeds and comment on their tweets. Don't overdo it to the point you look like a stalker, but interact regularly enough so that the journalists you're courting see you as an expert — making it more likely they pay will attention to your story pitches. If they see you as a truly reliable and honest source, they may also start calling you for comments on stories in your field.

Share your expertise as a speaker

Seek out opportunities to speak to groups where there are likely to be prospective customers, such as industry conferences. You'll have to begin small at local chapters of larger organizations, but stairstep your way to the national stage by demonstrating your chops at local appearances. Use videos of these speeches to pitch larger venues. And be sure to invite journalists to your speaking engagements. (They are more likely to attend if you hint that you plan to say something surprising or announce big news,)

Write a column for your local newspaper

The economic squeeze the news business is enduring means that many publications – especially small, community newspapers – are hurting for content. If you're in a consumer-focused industry, such as law, accounting, healthcare or home maintenance, pitch your local paper on running a regular column in which you provide helpful advice within your area of expertise.

Submit articles to guest posting sites

Unlike most news outlets, where you must contact an editor or reporter and convince them to use your information, many news sites make it easy to submit articles for publication – even providing a form you can use. Some good ones include Outbrain and HubSpot, for articles about marketing; Investopedia, for articles about finance; Sitepoint, for articles about technology; and Lifehack, if you're an expert on productivity. There are many others. Just search for "guest posting" to find them. Getting published on these sites helps establish your credibility, giving you links you can use to bolster your SEO (search engine optimization).

Share your expertise via LinkedIn

Commit to writing and posting at least one LinkedIn longform post a month on a topic where you can offer unique insights. Then join LinkedIn groups that pertain to that topic; promote your posts there and comment on posts by others in the group.

Become a Quora expert

Becoming a Quora expert takes a significant investment of time, and you must really know what you are talking about, but if you can meet these criteria, it can go a long way to raising your profile as an expert in your field. The key is to focus exclusively on topics in which you have deep knowledge and to provide detailed, fact-based answers. Canadian clinical psychologist Jordan Peterson followed this route to international fame as a "public intellectual."

Is doing your own PR a lot of work? Yes. Does it take a long-term commitment? Yes. Is it worth it? Yes, because it is the best way to draw attention and customers to your business — and grow your revenue to the point that you can hire a professional PR firm to do this hard work for you.

- Originally appeared in Forbes

Five Reasons to Fire Your PR Firm

We sometimes face the challenge of dealing with the trauma inflicted on prospective clients by other PR firms. Having been burned once, these skittish prospects are understandably reluctant to try it again — even though they realize their company needs a well-orchestrated public relations effort.

Now, it is not every day we hear complaints about other PR firms. In my experience, the vast majority of our competitors, both regionally and nationally, are upstanding citizens who do what they say they will do. However, there are obviously a few bad apples, because we hear about them.

*Does your PR firm simply react to what you ask for
rather than bring ideas to you?
If so, you've hired an expensive messenger service, not a PR firm.*

I'd like to get the bad apples out of our profession, but this will only happen when people stop hiring them, or at least fire them quickly. This means that business owners must be able to recognize quickly when they've hired an underperforming PR firm. Following is a checklist for doing so.

1. Very little happens for the first few months of your engagement

Bad apples will tell you that PR takes time and not to expect results right away, which is correct, to a point. It does take time to put a new program into place — but it will never happen if there is little to no activity. If your goal is to generate publicity, and your new PR firm has not written and pitched at least a couple of press releases within the first two months of your engagement — fire them. If they've not met with you and laid out their publicity plan — fire them. If they have not generated a single news story and can't tell you what reporters are telling them — fire them, because they likely haven't talked to any reporters.

In short, if you get a lot of excuses and no results the first few months, they are either lazy or don't know what they are doing, or both. Fire them.

2. You are not kept informed about what they are doing

We use regular client meetings to showcase the work we've done and outline the work we plan to carry out next month. Of course, between these meetings, emails and phone calls are traded back and forth for interviews, strategy discussions, copy approval and other topics.

If communication with your PR firm consists primarily of them sending you a monthly invoice, then chances are they have nothing to talk about. Fire them.

3. You must tell them what to do

Are you telling your PR firm what press releases to write, blogs to post or social media content to generate? Do they simply react to what you ask for rather than bring ideas to you? If so, you've hired an expensive messenger service, not a PR firm. Fire them

4. They do not understand your industry

We will never understand a client's industry as well as they do, but we will know more about it than anyone not in the industry — because we immerse ourselves in it, visiting competitors' websites, talking with journalists who cover the industry, following industry Twitter feeds and setting up alerts to stay on top of developments. If you still must explain the basics of your industry to your PR firm after working with them for a couple of months, fire them. If they haven't made the effort to understand what you do, how are they going to convince your target markets to care?

5. They do the same things, regardless of your industry

Of course, not all bad apples are indolent. Some are very busy, but busy about the wrong things. That's because they have one prescription to fix everything. For example, does your new PR firm automatically say you need a Facebook page without first learning something about your customers? See "They do not understand your industry" above. If all they have is a hammer, every problem looks like a nail to them.

Fire them, before you get hammered.

Lessons From the Father of Public Relations

Edward Bernays, the self-proclaimed "Father of Public Relations," realized a fundamental truth of effective PR: people are more likely to believe your story if it is told by someone else.

Draft off the power of societal trends

While many, if not most, men smoked in the early 20th Century, it was still taboo for women. The tobacco industry hired Bernays to overcome this restriction in the market.

> *People are more likely to believe your story*
> *if it is told by someone else.*

The suffrage movement was in full swing and the inequality of men and women was on the public's mind. Bernays surmised that breaking the taboo of women smoking in public could make a statement about women's desire to be treated equally, and thus, play into the current national narrative.

Bernays hired fashionable women to walk in the 1929 New York City Easter Parade smoking a cigarette — and alerted the press about this scandalous display of feminine independence. It became a national story and women began being seen in public openly smoking what Bernays dubbed "torches of freedom."

Lesson: Leverage societal trends to tap into the deep well of emotions driving such trends. But be aware that you risk alienating those who think differently. People's feelings about society and culture are strong and deep-rooted.

Tap into the fascination of fashion

Also in the early 20th Century, Lucky Strike cigarettes was having a challenging time convincing women to buy a pack of Luckys because women were put off by the pack's forest green color. Lucky Strike hired Bernays to change women's opinion of the color.
Bernays researched green and learned it is the symbol of "hope,

victory and plenty." *(See "The Color of Money" chapter for more on the science of color.)* Using this information, he wrote to fashion designers and department stores urging them to promote the color and found success. Soon, store window displays featured "Lucky Strike" green.

He also staged an important fashion event called The Green Ball. An "unnamed sponsor" (Lucky Strike) made a donation in the names of the leading women who came to the ball in green gowns. At the invitation of Bernays, the major fashion magazines covered the event.

Lesson: Your product or service need have nothing to do with fashion to cozy up to the panache it offers. Be creative.

Buy experts to tout your message

When the nation's biggest producer of bacon called on Bernays to help them sell more pork, Bernays sought out an authoritative outsider to make his client's case — though, as was the case with most "outsiders" Bernays relied upon, it was someone in his employ.

When Bernays asked his on-retainer physician if a hearty breakfast of bacon and eggs would be healthier than the lighter fare most American's were consuming at the time, the doctor unsurprisingly agreed. When Bernays asked him to get other doctors to concur, more than 5,000 physicians agreed that a big breakfast of bacon and eggs was "scientifically desirable." The results of this survey of bacon-loving doctors were distributed to news media across the nation, who eagerly shared the news.

Lesson: Pay experts to say nice things about your product or service, and to get other experts to agree.

Create your own credibility-enhancing organizations

When Bernays could not find or buy an existing authoritative source to endorse his clients' products, he created his own out of thin air, such as the Committee for the Study and Promotion of the Sanitary Dispensing of Food and Drink, which he devised to sell more Dixie Cups. This self-created authority spread the message that it was safter to drink from disposable paper cups than reusable cups.

With this campaign, Bernays proved that an "authoritative source" which you create yourself can be just as effective as a real, objective authority if you promote it heavily enough.

Lesson: If you want your message to have more credibility, create a credible-sounding organization to communicate the message.

Do in-depth, wide-ranging research to find messages others miss

In the early 20th Century, only women wore wristwatches. Men used pocket watches and those who wore wristwatches were suspected of being homosexual. Once again, Bernays sought an outside authority who could convincingly communicate the message he wanted believed – that "real men" wore wrist watches.

He discovered that it was dangerous for American soldiers to carry a pocket watch during battle, because when they lit a match to see it, they became a target. Using this research, he convinced the U.S. Army that wristwatches could save soldiers' lives. Wristwatches became standard issue in the Army, a very masculine occupation, and therefore wiping out the taboo against men wearing wrist watches.

Lesson: Look for the unexpected in your product research and talk to the people who are using it to find these "real life" stories. No one would have ever connected pocket watches with personal danger if Bernays had not conducted such thorough and wide-ranging research.

Publicity is more effective than advertising because a message about a product appears to come from an independent source, the news media. Bernays discovered that it is even more effective to put another layer of credibility between your product and the news media – an outside authority, even if you create and manage such an authority yourself.

- Originally appeared in Forbes

Lessons From the Roman Empire

If Rome, especially Roman emperors, had done more of the right things and less of the wrong ones, we might all be speaking Latin today. The things Rome did right and did wrong parallel the things marketers do right and wrong.

Want to conquer the market? Take these lessons from ancient Rome:

Meet basic needs first

Roman emperors realized they could do pretty much what they wanted if they kept Romans well-fed and entertained, i.e., the "bread and circuses" approach to governing, in which Romans were guaranteed an allotment of grain and a regular diet of gladiatorial contests, mock battles and Christians being fed to lions.

> *Don't try to change his beliefs so they better fit*
> *what your product offers.*
> *Meet him where he is, on his turf.*

Similarly, the savvy marketer will make sure that she addresses her customers' basic informational needs before trying anything elaborate. For example, an informative and intuitive website is foundational to any digital marketing campaign. Also foundational to many marketing programs is a public relations program that raises awareness and establishes credibility.

Meet people where they are

When Romans conquered a country and added it to the empire, they did not try to impose Roman ways on the conquered. The vanquished were allowed to keep their religion (though Caesar was often added to the local pantheon) as well as their customs, their holidays and their way of life — while simultaneously receiving the substantial benefits of Roman citizenship. The only thing required was that the new citizens pay taxes to Rome (nobody ever escapes taxes) and that a portion of the male population serve in the Roman Army — to bring more people into the empire.

The lesson here is pretty basic: spend a lot of effort getting to know your customer, what makes him tick, then show him how your product relates to the way he ticks — and helps him tick better, faster, more beautifully. Don't try to change his beliefs so they better fit what your product offers. Meet him where he is, on his turf, by showing how your product reinforces his beliefs.

And, though you can't conscript an army, you can recruit ambassadors who broaden your reach. Use extraordinary service to transform customers into ambassadors, or bribe your army of ambassadors with free products and experiences.

Don't forget existing customers

There are many theories about why Rome fell. One is that Roman leaders were too busy expanding the empire to pay attention to what was happening at home. Some emperors rarely set foot in the Eternal City throughout their entire reign.

Sometimes, a company makes this same mistake when the leadership focuses more on winning new business than on keeping existing customers. From a marketing standpoint, the biggest violation of this rule is offering new customers a better deal than existing customers have. It's amazing how often this happens.

Have a great story

Rome had not one, but two great creation myths. One, that the city was founded by two brothers, Romulus and Remus, who were children of a god and a virgin and were raised by wolves. (I mean, can you get any better than that?) The other is that the city traces its roots back to one of the greatest cities in ancient history, Troy, whereby Aeneas — the leader of a band of Trojan princes who escaped Greece's sack of their city — founded Rome as a new home for his royal band. (Slightly more believable, but still fabulous.)

Both these stories reinforced Rome's reputation as a country of godlike, strong, resourceful, clever, unrelenting and ruthless people who are destined for greatness.

Like Rome, great companies have a compelling story. Apple's is that it was founded by a godlike, strong, resourceful, clever, unrelenting and ruthless man who bent the world to his will by selling products we didn't know we needed until Apple invented them – kind of like the godlike Romans who bestowed Roman citizenship on people who didn't know there was any other way to live.

Here are some others, from our clients:

- Turner Construction's story is that its founder not only invented the reinforced concrete building and thereby transformed the world's built environment, but did so because Mr. Turner believed deeply in quality, hard work and responsiveness to client needs.

- First Tennessee Bank's story is that it was founded during the Civil War and has been helping people overcome adversity ever since, including two World Wars, a yellow fever epidemic, the Great Depression, the Great Recession and the Great Pandemic. It's a story about strength and compassion.

- The Bradford Group's story is that we are a company founded by strong, resourceful, creative and unrelenting people which evolved into a team that balances the drive to succeed with compassion, openness, humor and respect.

What's your story?

Lessons From Russia's Master Propagandist

I'm always on the lookout for successful political propagandists because they are often at the vanguard of public relations. That's how I discovered Vladislav Surkov, the maestro behind the rise of Vladimir Putin and the propaganda campaign that paved the way for Russia's invasion of Ukraine in 2022.

> *Effecting change without creating the perception*
> *that anything has changed*
> *is the epitome of successful propaganda/PR.*

This chapter summarizes key propaganda techniques that Surkov invented or perfected. I am not advocating these tactics. Indeed, they require the absolute control possible only in a totalitarian state. But I believe it's possible to learn valuable lessons from any master of his art, even if the master's intentions are unsavory.

Create your own reality

Similar to the "big lie" technique pioneered by another master propagandist, Joseph Goebbels, Surkov advocates inventing a reality that suits your ends and imposing it on the population. An excellent example is Surkov's creation of Novorossiya, the name he gave to a wedge of southeastern Ukraine. Novorossiya means literally "New Russia," telegraphing Surkov's and Putin's feelings about where this region belongs.

As the *Atlantic* magazine noted in a September 2014 article about Surkov, "The term [Novorossiya] is plucked from tsarist history, when it represented a different geographical space. Nobody who lives in that part of the world today ever thought of themselves as living in Novorossiya and bearing allegiance to it — at least until several months ago. Now, Novorossiya is being imagined into being: Russian media are showing maps of its 'geography,' while Kremlin-backed politicians are writing its 'history' into school textbooks. There's a flag and even a news agency (in English and Russian). There are several Twitter feeds."

Set the stage — and let the desired script play out

Surkov spent time in the theater, which likely shaped his penchant for letting the reality you want "create itself" — like the self-directed story of a reality show. (Surkov admits he learns a lot from American reality shows.) Though he certainly has told journalists exactly what to write, he usually employs a lighter touch. To him, the most effective political theater involves setting the stage — establishing the Big Lie guiding the public conversation — and then seeding the conflicts from which the results you want will flow. The results then naturally feed back into the system, continuing without much intervention by the propagandist.

Financial Times quotes Surkov as saying, "People need to see themselves on stage. In this masked comedy, there is a director, there is a plot. And this is when I understood what needed to be done. We had to give diversity to people. But that diversity had to be under control. And then everyone would be satisfied. And at the same time, the unity of the society would be preserved... It works, this model works. It is a good compromise between chaos and order."

And in *Almost Zero*, a novel about a propagandist that Surkov wrote under a pseudonym, Surkov says of the protagonist, "His shadows, his puppets, his imagination, were all controlled by the audience, not his own self." Once the stage is set and the plot begun, the actors and the audience unknowingly create the script and act it out.

Create and manage your own opposition

In Surkov's world, creating realities should not be limited to spreading sweetness and light. In fact, the most important reality to create is your opposition — because you can control what you create, while still giving the perception that people are freely debating the issues.

Conflict is essential to move the play forward. A talented propagandist does not attempt to quash opposition; he creates it and manages it.

Surkov told the *Financial Times*, "When I started my work in 2000, I suggested a very simple system to bring law and order. We split the opposition into systemic and non-systemic. And what is systemic opposition? That is one that obeys the rules, laws and customs."

And as the *Atlantic* noted in November 2014: "Surkov would sit behind a desk with phones bearing the names of all the 'independent' party leaders, calling and directing them at any moment, day or night. The brilliance of this new type of authoritarianism is that instead of simply oppressing opposition, as had been the case with 20th-century strains, it climbs inside all ideologies and movements, exploiting and rendering them absurd."

Maintain appearances while changing everything

The real secret to Surkov's technique is casting a blanket of normality over the entire Hieronymus Bosch landscape he is creating. In this way, he mimics a ruler who may have been the first and greatest propagandist of all time: Caesar Augustus (known as Octavian when he had newly ascended to the throne of Rome). Surkov said:

"Octavian came to power when the nation, the people, were wary of fighting. He created a different type of state. It was not a republic anymore ... he preserved the formal institutions of the republic — there was a senate, there was a tribune. But everyone reported to one person and obeyed him. Thus, he married the wishes of the republicans who killed Caesar, and those of the common people who wanted a direct dictatorship.

"Putin did the same with democracy. He did not abolish it. He married it with the monarchical archetype of Russian governance. This archetype is working. It is not going anywhere... It has enough freedom and enough order."

Lessons from a master (monster)

So, what lessons can we mere capitalists learn from this totalitarian master propagandist? I think we learn that an effective communication strategy should clearly state the reality it believes in and seek to bring it into existence. That we name this reality, give it life, imbue it with emotional significance and, in fact, insist that it exists.

We also learn that indirection can be more effective than directed action. *(See chapter "Lessons from the Father of Public Relations" for more on this topic.)* It is often best to choose the main players, set the stage, outline the parameters of what matters and why, and then let the action play out to generate the result you seek without obviously changing anything. Effecting change without creating the perception that anything has changed is the epitome of successful propaganda/PR.

- Originally appeared in O'Dwyer's PR magazine

Lessons From the British Royal Family

In 2022, a monarch is head of state in 43 countries. Yet one royal family stands alone in relevance and influence: the Windsors of Great Britain. Fascination with the British royal family pervades even countries founded on anti-monarchial principles, i.e., the United States.

The British royal family have done an excellent job
of building a brand that resonates with most people, British or not.

Why is that? I suggest it is good PR. The British royal family — "The Firm," as they call themselves — has done an excellent job for decades of using public relations tactics to build and maintain a brand that resonates with most people, whether they are British or not. Pretty good for an outmoded institution, but how have they done this?

Maintain consistency of message

Rule #1 in public relations is consistency of message. This applies not only to what you say, but to what you don't say. The Windsors have been notoriously strict about staying on message for decades, a message summed up by Queen Elizabeth II in her inaugural address to the British Commonwealth in 1947: "I declare before you all that my whole life, whether it be long or short, shall be devoted to your service and the service of our great imperial family to which we all belong." The royal image is conservative, respectful, considerate, humble yet strong — the archetypical servant leader.

This message guides not just what royals say, but what they don't say and how they act. For example, lest they appear partisan, no member of the royal family is allowed to vote or to publicly express their opinion about political matters. Lest they appear flashy, they must adhere to a conservative dress code — down to the color of nail polish women can wear. (Only clear or pink.) They must accept all gifts they receive with graciousness, no matter how unwanted. *(See "The Reciprocity Principle" chapter in this book.)* And they can't play Monopoly because, as Prince Andrew once noted, it brings out their vicious side.

Lesson: Be clear about what you and your business stand for. Write out three to four talking points that sum up your brand and stick to them. And walk your talk: don't do anything that goes against your stated values.

Partner with the right people and brands

Except for the abdicated Edward VIII, who publicly associated with Nazis, the Windsors have always been very astute with whom they associate their brand. Formally, this is done via Royal Warrants of Appointment, which gives the manufacturer the right to mark his product with the royal arms and the statement, "By appointment to His Majesty the King," implying that the product is literally fit for a king. Over 800 entities have Royal Warrant of Appointment today, all the finest quality, as befits the royal family's image.

They have also put together other, more imaginative partnerships, such as Queen Elizabeth's joint video appearance with Paddington Bear to promote her Platinum Jubilee. The video gave The Firm an opportunity to showcase the queens' kindness, thoughtfulness and sense of humor — all on-brand — and connect the royal brand with a national symbol beloved by people of all classes and backgrounds. (Thousands of Paddington Bears joined the many flowers left outside royal residences in London following the queen's death in 2022.)

Then there was the quite funny and well-done partnership with "James Bond" — another symbol of British skill and daring — during which the queen appeared to parachute from a helicopter with actor Daniel Craig onto the field to start the London Olympics. Also very much on-brand, this outrageous stunt positioned the queen and Britain's monarchy as proud of the country's adventurous history and also smart and self-confident enough to do something so over-the-top.

Lesson: You can enhance your brand by drafting off the equity of other well-known and respected brands, but carefully consider every partnership to assure it presents an image consistent with the image you have crafted.

Adapt to the times

Beyond seeking out contemporary partners, from Paddington Bear to James Bond, the British royal family has done an excellent job of adapting its brand to the changing times — most dramatically demonstrated by King George V's changing of the family name in 1917. The problem was the British royal family's German origin, obvious from its Teutonic surname: Sax-Cobert Gotha. (At the time, Britain was being assaulted by German "Gotha G. IV" heavy bomber planes.) George simply declared the family's name to be the very British-sounding Windsor, the name of one of the family's English castles. Public dissatisfaction with having a German on the throne of England dissipated.

Lesson: Though consistency of message is important, stay tuned to the winds of change and have the foresight and courage to make a change when external circumstances put your brand in danger.

To find the royal road to brand success, consider adopting the servant-ruler ways of the British royal family. It's not easy (though they make it look so), but if you combine conservatism with bold moves like they have done for literally a thousand years, you may find yourself head of a commercial dynasty.

- Originally appeared in Forbes

Lessons From a Horrible, Terrible, No-Good Year

I think it's safe to say that 2020 – the year of the COVID pandemic – ties with 1929 as one of the worst years the world has endured in modern times. But whatever doesn't kill us makes us smarter. This chapter mines 2020 for lessons that PR professionals can use to be more effective.

Everyone has their own reality

While the pandemic was a worldwide crisis, each person had a unique experience with it. Some suffered incalculable loss, and some struggled but recovered, while others were affected only tangentially, if at all. The varied experiences were filtered through each person's cultural background, personality, political views and other factors.

If cultural values aren't respected and understood,
everyone is less likely to understand the motivations
behind what people say and do.

Thus, there are vastly different perspectives on current events, and they influence the way people react. These individual realities must be respected, not argued with, if you hope to communicate – or accomplish anything.

Authority matters

Early on, we realized that one way to judge the reliability of information is to judge the authority of the entity from which it emanates. Factors determining authority are the issuing entity's length of existence, history of accuracy, depth of resources, insulation from partisan forces and moderation of tone – factors worth keeping in mind post-pandemic, tempered by the fact that virtually no organization emerged from the pandemic with enhanced authority.

Anything can be politicized

Who would have thought, pre-pandemic, that medical advice could be political? We now know that virtually anything can be fraught with political overtones, even something as mundane as a face mask. What matters is what you do with a thing (like, mandate it), versus what the thing is.

Social media can only confirm beliefs, not change them

Though few political views have ever been changed via any means of communication, the peculiarities of social media — the truncated responses, the ability to selectively respond, the anonymity — make it a space in which attempts at political conversion are especially futile. Because discussions about the pandemic were invariability political, those that transpired on social media only hardened beliefs. We should always keep this limitation of social media in mind.

Cultural differences hinder communication

Quite simply, if cultural values aren't respected and understood, everyone is less likely to understand the motivations behind what people say and do and, thus, less likely to believe what's being said is true and valid. In America during the pandemic, this cultural dissonance and communications disconnect was most obvious between urban and rural populations.

Predictions are unpredictable

Based on results from China, which experienced the pandemic sooner than the rest of the world, and which has a more authoritarian culture that allowed for a more drastic and universal response in fighting it, many experts (though certainly not all) predicted that the virus would largely run its course within a few months. It didn't. This reminds us to always take predictions with a grain of salt.

Policies resolve unsolvable problems

When we find ourselves in a politically fraught situation, where choosing sides will invariably lead to angering a generous portion of people, the best course of action is to establish a policy and stick to it. Consistency is an effective defense against the vagaries of public opinion.

Proximal problems compound effects

In Nashville, we were hit in 2020 with the pandemic, then a devastating tornado, then a huge truck bomb that destroyed an especially historic — and, thus, irreplaceable — section of downtown. Having several disasters occurring relatively close together compounded the effect of each one. The tornado seemed worse because it occurred during an unprecedented pandemic. The bomb — on Christmas morning! — had a deeper, more wrenching effect because it came at the end of such a horrible year.

Artificial boundaries can have real effects

January 1, 2021 was really no different than December 31, 2020 — we crossed an abstract, artificial boundary. But it felt like a renewal. We were more optimistic about the future in early 2021. And we fared better in 2021 simply because we moved one more time around the sun — not because anything was materially different.

The people alive today may never (hopefully) experience another year like 2020. Though it was horrendous, 2020 can be a valuable experience if we take time to sift through the pain for lessons we can apply in more "normal" times — because, though times change, people remain the same. The character traits, the communication patterns, the biases, the courage and graciousness that emerge in times of stress will always be there, just below the surface. We'll be better, stronger, smarter, kinder and more successful if we keep this in mind.

- Originally appeared in Forbes

The Good, The Bad and The Operative: Propaganda Types and Uses

In this chapter, we'll explore the main propaganda techniques developed since the birth of modern public relations in WWI and advise on how the leaders of organizations today can make the best use of these techniques to advance their interests.

Propaganda encompasses a range of tactics – all of which are effective, and many of which are ethical.

Propaganda techniques fall in seven categories:, three positive, three negative and an operative (biological, psychological) category.

The three positive categories of propaganda are **Belonging, Transferring** and **Authoritative**. Belonging tactics meet our need to find meaning through other people. Through Transferring techniques, we project qualities – either good or bad – onto others. And Authoritative actions rely on our somewhat ingrained response to submit to authority, or to at least give it its due.

The three negative categories are **Lying, Blurring** and **Othering**. Lying is communicating false information and generally creating confusion to change the accepted version of reality. Blurring is "spinning" the message to emphasize a point or obscure it. And Othering techniques amplify our tendency to blame others for our problems, often (preferably) people we do not know.

The **Operative** category includes techniques that trigger reflexive actions based on what psychologist Daniel Kahneman called System 1 thinking. *(See chapter "The Psychology of Public Relations: Fast and Slow.")* Though they may be used for moral or immoral purposes, in themselves operative techniques are amoral, like any biologically automatic process.

Propaganda techniques in the Belonging category are:

- **Bandwagon,** which taps into our need for "social proof," i.e., that something must be worth doing if everyone is doing it. Both Barack Obama and Donald Trump used this technique in their presidential campaigns. Obama created a bandwagon vision of "hope and change;" Trump promoted a vision of regaining America's past glory. Both visions were cast as the future that you want to be part of, lest you miss the boat.

- **Common Man,** which cloaks the propagandist's purposes in the language and concerns of everyday people so that the ideas are more acceptable. Again, the best examples come from presidential politics. Four of the last five presidents — Biden, Trump, Bush, Clinton — cast themselves as regular guys.

- **Flag-waving,** which ties the propagandist's campaign to patriotism and the positive feelings it arouses. The gun industry is most likely to warp itself in the flag, or more specifically, the Constitution's Second Amendment. Gun ads are replete with eagles and flags. Marketing for pickup trucks and off-road vehicles is also openly patriotic: both Jeep and Chevy claim to sell "American Tough" machines.

  - *How to use Belonging techniques:* Use belonging techniques liberally. They are fully accepted, even lauded, promotional techniques in American society. You will be hard-pressed to find a company that has not used them.

    Ethically, belonging techniques are also the most transparent and "democratic" methods of convincing people to believe something. Everyone knows that the barker for the bandwagon is selling a show; injecting a common touch into your presentation is simply courtesy and good sense; and nothing can be more transparent than an appeal to patriotism — its obviousness is what makes it effective.

Propaganda techniques in the Transferring category are:

- **Virtue Signaling,** in which the propagandist inserts into his message concepts that are widely acclaimed – like "diverse" or "sustainable" or "ESG" – to transfer the positive associations of these concepts to his cause. This, of course, is rampant today: Nike aligning with Black Lives Matter, Disney fighting for LGBTI+ rights, and all the companies who assured us "they are with us" during the COVID pandemic.

- **Beautiful People,** in which you get attractive, talented, wealthy or otherwise appealing people to endorse your product, causing people to unconsciously believe that they will also be a "beautiful person" if they buy your product. This has long been the most-used marketing / propaganda technique. There is even an industry to support it: the spokesperson and model industry. The outbreak of Influentials marketing is based on the power of this propaganda technique.

  - *How to use Transferring techniques:* Again, use them liberally. They work quite well, and no one will call you out for stating virtuous platitudes or having a celebrity endorse your product – unless your celebrity is openly political, then tread carefully, because the customers the celebrity scares off may outnumber those attracted. For instance, the jury is still out on Nike's association with NFL player Colin Kaepernick, famous as one of the first professional athletes to kneel in protest when the national anthem was played before a game began. There were lots of social media posts of burning shoes, but the company's stock rose 5% in the weeks after the Kaepernick ad ran.

Propaganda techniques in the Authoritative category are:

- **Appeal to Authority,** in which someone whom people normally obey, or at least respect, endorses your product. The most direct appeal to authority in the world is the Royal Warrant of Appointment granted by British royalty, which attests to the quality of goods and services used by the crown as literally fit for a king. *(See chapter "Lessons From the British Royal Family.)*

- **Direct Order** and **Testimonial** are types of appeal to authority. One involves the authority figure telling people to do something, such as, "Uncle Sam Wants You" (to join the Army). The other involves the authority figure putting her reputation on the line for your product.

  - *How to use Authoritative techniques:* Use them whenever you can identify an authoritative person in your industry and can convince or pay that person to endorse you. However, there must be a genuine connection between your product and the authority figure, that is, her story must mesh with yours in some way. For example, Greta Thunberg would be a marvelous brand representative for Patagonia, but the same would not hold for Dow Chemical.

Propaganda techniques in the Lying category are:

- **The Big Lie,** in which repeated references are made to a largely invented circumstance that becomes the basis and justification for a course of action. The most famous Big Lie was Hitler's assertion that the Jews were to blame for all of Germany's problems. In fact, Hitler and his minister of propaganda, Joseph Goebbels, coined the term "Big Lie." In *Mein Kampf*, Hitler wrote, "The great masses of the people... will more easily fall victim to a big lie than to a small one." Goebbels wrote, "If you tell a lie big enough and keep repeating it, people will eventually come to believe it.

- **Disinformation,** which is creating communications — news reports, movies, books, etc. — that alter the facts about what happened. Today, disinformation is also known as fake news, and examples are legion: that Pope Francis endorsed Donald Trump for president, that China stole the coronavirus from Canada and weaponized it, that the Clintons used a pizza restaurant as a front for a child sex ring, and on and on. Perhaps the most famous, and chilling, example of disinformation is the Ministry of Truth in George Orwell's book *1984*, where news reports were continually "updated" to support the current "reality" that government wished people to believe.

- **Half-Truths** is altering the truth in such a way that, even though it is wrong, it incorporates enough of the truth to make it difficult to automatically reject. For example, a friend calls to tell you that she just drove by your house and noticed that your mailbox is damaged — but omits mentioning that she hit your mailbox with your car.

- **Quotes Out of Context** attempts to use quotes by respected people in a context that make it appear they are saying something other than what they intended. This technique is often used in book blurbs and movie trailers. For example, a blurb might state that a certain reviewer thought a book was "Fantastic," whereas what he really said was that the book is "a fantastic amalgamation of lies and shoddy research."

  - *How to use Lying techniques:* Do NOT use these techniques. They are evil. You will inevitably be worse off than if you did nothing.

Propaganda techniques in the Blurring category are:

- **Glittering Generalities, Oversimplification** and **Obfuscation,** all of which involve highlighting the positive and ignoring the negative, and generally painting a vaguely happy picture of what you are doing and how it affects people. An example is the oversimplification that "School violence has gone up and academic performance has gone down since video games featuring violence were introduced" – which assumes that problems in schools are due to a single cause.

- **Red Herring, Straw Man** and **Rationalization**, which involve raising side issues that have little to do with your situation to draw attention away from your problems. The Red Herring is an unrelated distraction. The Straw Man is a manufactured problem that you claim to overcome. Rationalization uses favorable generalities to justify questionable ends. These techniques are favorites of politicians who wish to change the topic when they are asked a difficult question. For example, a member of congress is accused of corruption and, instead of responding to the charge, he points to the amount of federal dollars that has flowed to his district during his term.

- **The Black-or-White Fallacy** attempts to reduce complex issues to simple "yes or no" questions, with the propagandist's "yes" put forth as the obvious response. For example, the statement "Love it or leave it," heard often from conservative groups during the 1960s when left-leading groups were questioning American policies and values, posits that one is either 100% for America or 100% against it, and the obvious "right" response is "love it." Of course, this ignores the many shades of patriotism that exist, including the possibility that someone's love of the country leads them to question certain government policies. The so-called "cancel culture" that pervades many college campuses today is another example of the black-or-white fallacy, in which leftist political views are deemed 100% correct and rightest views are 100% incorrect, thus worthy of suppressing.

  o *How to use Blurring techniques:* In fact, it is hard not to use most of these techniques, as simplifying the message and emphasizing the positive is ingrained into marketing. People would probably be confused to see the whole, unembellished truth in a commercial communication.

Propaganda techniques in the Othering category are:

- **Appealing to Fear, Demonizing the Enemy, Ad Hominem Attacks** and **Scapegoating,** all of which attempt to project our fears onto others and then banish/attack the other to overcome our fears. Whenever social media interaction turns to politics, you're sure to find these tactics in use — with claims that the other side is "destroying democracy," or that the person espousing a disagreeable opinion is an immoral person, or claiming that all of our problems are due to one group of people.

- **Labeling** and **Name-Calling** use words to make it clear that the other is the problem. Labelling is applying existing negative political terms — like "liberal" or "Nazi" — to our enemy. Name calling is describing the enemy negatively, like "creepy," "idiot" or "mentally ill."

- **Appeal to Prejudice** and **Stereotyping** tap into the negative emotions we have about certain groups of people to turn us against them, or toward the propagandists' interests.

  - *How to use Othering techniques:* Don't use them. Though they can be effective in the short term, especially for manipulating crowd psychology, they are disastrous over the long term because the slime of these tactics clings to reputations.

Propaganda techniques in the Operative category are:

- **Cognitive Dissonance,** which plays on our need to be consistent. For example, if a propagandist finds that people hate his candidate but love a particular actor, he can use the actor's endorsement of his candidate to change people's minds because we can't abide inconsistency. We are forced to either dislike the actor or like the candidate.

- **Classical Conditioning,** in which the propagandist taps into our innate propensity to associate a prompt with an effect when they are presented together. For example, if news reports of violence always include references to a particular race, we will associate that race with violence.

- **Latitudes of Acceptance.** If the propagandist's message is unacceptable to most people, he can make it more acceptable by either communicating a more extreme position that will make his original position seem more moderate, or he can moderate his position and then alter it over time until it is aligns with the original position.

- **Reciprocity,** which plays on our ingrained need to respond in-kind when someone gives us a gift or does us a favor. *(See "The Reciprocity Principle" chapter in this book.)*

- **Ad Nauseum,** the unrelenting repetition of a statement, slogan, motto, etc. until it is taken as the truth. You can see this tactic at work anytime you see politicians of the same party repeating the same talking point over and over, regardless of the question they are asked.

  - *How to use Operative techniques:* People are cynically used to them and by and large simply accept these techniques as part of how the world works. However, as with any powerful tool or weapon, these tactics can backfire in the hands of amateurs who lack the sophistication and subtly of professionals.

Propaganda got a bad name in World War II because of its use by the Nazis. (Of course, both sides in the war made heavy use of propaganda.) The fact is that propaganda encompasses a range of tactics — all of which are effective, and many of which are ethical. The marketer's job is to sift through the Machiavellian morass to find the propaganda techniques that will make your job easier without making your company a villain.

- Originally appeared in Forbes

The Psychology of Public Relations: Fast and Slow

We have long known that people are a combination of at least two different selves. The Greeks identified them as Apollo and Dionysus: the god of reason and light, and the god of emotion and darkness. Freud called them the ego and the id: our rational conscious self and our irrational unconscious self. St. Paul called them spirit and flesh.

No matter what you call them, these two facets of your being exist, and how they interact largely determines who you are and what you do.

Professor Kahneman has recast the age-old marketing premise that our buying decisions are based on emotion, but we use reason to justify them.

In *Thinking: Fast and Slow* psychologist and economist Daniel Kahneman does an incredible job of analyzing our Apollonian and Dionysian natures and providing a roadmap (perhaps inadvertently) that marketers can use to chart the route of prospective customers to a sale.

His basic premise is that we have two ways of interacting with the world: System 1, which is how we automatically process information, and System 2, which is effortful thinking about objective facts. They roughly correspond to Dionysus (id) and Apollo (ego).

The job of a marketer is to tap into System 1, preferably by simultaneously convincing the prospect that he is being guided by System 2 — which is not at all difficult, as we frequently think we are using System 2 when we are actually being led by System 1.

Here's an example, drawn from his book, of how this is done:

You see a person reading the *New York Times* on the New York subway. Which of the following is most likely?

- She has a PhD.

- She does not have a college degree.

Most of us (including me) would bet on the PhD, because this coincides with our intuitive impression that people who read the *Times* are likely to be well-educated. Furthermore, if asked how we arrived at this conclusion, we would say that we thoughtfully considered what is most likely to be true, that is, that we used System 2. Statistically, however, we are likely to be wrong, because there are many more non-college graduates than PhDs — so it's likely our *Times* reader does not have a college degree.

If you chose PhD, you were using System 1, which, under many cases, is not a bad way to get along in the world. For example, if you believe that most people who act friendly are indeed friendly and that young men are more likely than elderly women to drive aggressively, you'll be right in most cases — but not always, and you could be led far astray from the truth.

Professor Kahneman points out that the movie *Moneyball* is an example of how people can be led astray by System 1 thinking. Traditional baseball scouts forecast the success of recruits by their build and look, that is, by the scouts' experience of being around successful ballplayers. However, the hero of the book, Oakland A's manager Billy Beane, overruled his scouts and chose players instead by analyzing the statistics of their past performance — using System 2 — and he won ballgames.

In essence, what Professor Kahneman has done is recast the age-old marketing truism that our buying decisions are based on emotional factors, not rational ones — but that we use reason to retroactivity justify these decisions. He's just done it more elegantly and precisely.

Key lessons from the book are:

- Stereotypes work, particularly if the message is not obviously stereotypical, as in the "PhD subway" example.

- The law of least effort: thinking is hard and we don't do it unless we must. We are particularly likely to revert to System 1 when we are tired.

- When we are at ease, we are more receptive to information and more likely to accept what is said as true without reflection. When we are under strain, we are more likely to be vigilant and make fewer errors (but also be less creative).

- As a corollary to the above, effective messages should be simple, because understanding them takes less effort.

- If we believe a conclusion is true, we are likely to believe arguments that appear to support it, even when these arguments are unsound. (If System 1 is involved, the conclusions come first and the arguments follow.)

- Exposure to a word, concept or image primes us to think, feel and behave in a way consistent with this impression. For example, exposing people to images of classrooms and lockers increased their tendency to support a school initiative.

- "What You See Is All There Is:" We are predisposed to jump to conclusions based solely on the information in front of us. It is the consistency of the information that matters, not its completeness.

- When confronted with a difficult (System 2) question, we often substitute an easier (System 1) question without realizing it. For example, when asked, "How should financial advisors who prey on the elderly be punished?" we might unconsciously substitute and answer the simpler, System 1 question, "How much anger do I feel when I think of financial predators?"

Happy hunting.

Tesla Does Not Have a PR Department. Is That OK?

Elon Musk — the closest thing America has to a real, live John Galt — is always in the news. The funny thing is that the American capitalist with arguably the highest public profile in the world fired his entire PR department. This bold move was, as *Electrek* reported, "a new first in the industry." And, indeed, it is inconceivable that any other major company would operate this way.

In this PR pro's opinion, Musk is making a mistake, but like John Galt, he may have the last laugh.

About six months after dismantling Tesla's PR department, Musk doubled down on his decision and rejected the idea of bringing back the department because, per *Electrek*, "He doesn't believe in 'manipulating public opinion'" — which is odd coming from a fellow whose addiction to Twitter is legendary, whose Tweets have swayed national opinion and moved markets.

So, should Tesla have a PR department or not? We'll examine both sides in this chapter:

Why Tesla needs a PR department

- To provide reporters with accurate information

One of Musk's beefs with the news media is that he believes reporters report erroneous information about Tesla. One of the primary jobs of in-house public relations professionals is to provide journalists with verified, accurate information about the company, and to request corrections when incorrect information is published. This function alone seems like a compelling reason to bring back Tesla's PR department.

- To cultivate better relations with the press

Let's face it, journalists are people and, like everyone else, they have opinions — and their opinions may run counter to the story you want to tell. In my experience, you can increase your chances of fair coverage if you invest some time into getting to know the journalists who cover your company and industry. As one of the commentors on the *Electrek* story noted, "Press offices exist because of this reality. One of the elements of their work is developing a rapport with the people that cover your company/industry so that you get a fair shake."

- To nip negative stories in the bud — or at least get Tesla's side out

Again, in my experience, when you have established a relationship with the news media, reporters are much more likely to call you for comment on a negative story — and give you enough time to formulate a cogent response. And the fact is, journalists want to get it right; it's their reputation on the line, too.

- To prevent Musk from saying stupid things that hurt the brand

Musk has done some pretty dumb things on Twitter, such as calling a Thai rescue diver a "pedo guy." If Tesla had a policy that all official communication had to be run through the PR department, these kinds of needlessly damaging statements would not happen. Of course, this piece of advice applies to any CEO.

Why Tesla is fine without a PR department

- They sell cars as fast as they can make them

Frankly, if your company's sales are as robust as Tesla's, you should focus on meeting demand instead of trying to generate more of it.

- Musk is Tesla's PR department, and his cult of personality works for Tesla

In effect, Musk is a one-man PR department for Tesla who immediately communicates with everyone he needs to reach via Twitter. And, since the information is coming straight from the CEO, it's highly credible. However, it is a rare CEO who can do what Musk does. I've certainly never met one in my 35+ years of advising CEOs. Rather, I have seen companies destroyed by CEOs who thought they could say whatever they wanted, whenever they wanted, to whomever.

- Not having a PR dept makes Musk and Tesla look iconoclastic, which helps the brand

By forgoing a PR department, Tesla looks like a "different kind of company" that eschews the corporate ways of traditional, Detroit-based auto companies — which don't have a sterling reputation, overall. It also plays to Musk's cult-like status, which helps the brand.

- Musk can exaggerate with impunity because he has no accountability

Musk has been known to "overstate" facts about Tesla. For instance, he said that Tesla cars would be able to drive themselves anywhere, under any conditions, without human supervision, by the end of 2021 — a statement flatly contradicted by internal Tesla documents, as well as the bold facts of what did NOT happen. Without a PR department requiring public statements to be approved in advance, Musk is free to oversell Tesla with few repercussions.

Bottom Line: Though Tesla seems to be is doing fine without a PR department today, you never know what's around the corner. Assuring that a company is prepared for a crisis is a key responsibility of PR departments. Without this precaution in place, Tesla is vulnerable to a disaster that can't be handled with a Tweet from the CEO. But, more than this, though the company is successful today, who knows what opportunities it is missing because it turns a deaf ear to the news media. In this PR pro's opinion, Musk is making a mistake, but like John Galt, he may have the last laugh. Time will tell.

- Originally appeared in Forbes

Why Is Elon Musk Able to Own the Media?

I've been in the PR business almost 40 years, and I have never seen anyone own the news media like Elon Musk.

Here's a guy that can do something as stupid as Tweeting that a scuba diver trying to rescue Thai boys trapped in a flooded cave was a "pedo guy" — and emerge (eventually) reputation unscathed. (He took a temporary hit when he posted the Tweet, but the long-term damage to his reputation was nil.) Even though he is quite open about his libertarian political beliefs and unrepentantly disdainful of woke/DEI culture and other icons of progressive America that are widely supported by corporate America and national media, he is generally treated well by the national media, where he is basically portrayed as a sort of loveable mad scientist.

Think big. Accomplish much. Be honest and outspoken.
And embrace the whole you, not just the antiseptic parts.

The easy answer, of course, is that Musk is the world's richest man — and a privileged white guy, at that, from a wealthy family that owns an emerald mine, for gosh sakes — so it's no wonder he is a media darling. Come on: nothing is more laughable than claiming rich white guys are naturally treated well by the news media.

The fact that Musk is wealthy is an effect, not a cause. And I suggest that when we figure out the causes of his financial success, we'll have also identified the causes of his success in the media.

I believe the causes behind his success boil down to attitudes and beliefs that set him apart from his peers. And I believe that we ordinary mortals can learn from what Musk has done. Though we may not succeed on the same scale, I think that by adopting similar attitudes, we are more likely to succeed in the arena of public opinion, as well as in the marketplace.

These are the attitudes I think set Musk apart:

He sets his sights on big, inspirational goals

From creating the first commercially successful electric car company, to founding one of the first federally insured online banks, to colonizing Mars (two down, one to go), Musk tackles only huge, awe-inspiring projects.

The thing about amazing, inspiring goals is that people tend to get caught up in the altered reality in which the hero must operate to traffic in such outlandish goals. The public focus becomes less about the hero and his challenges, and more about the transformed reality he is living in. It makes for exceptional stories, and storytelling is the basis of all media relations and reputation management.

For the rest of us: find ways to add a bit of drama to your story by committing to doing something amazing. Propose to accomplish something that has never been accomplished, and do it.

He produces results

Musk created, funded and/or leads the most valuable car company in the world (Tesla), the most successful privately-owned space exploration company (SpaceX) and the world's leading online payment service (PayPay). He founded his first company, Zip2, when he was 24 years old and, four years later, sold his shares for $22 million.

His reputation would be non-existent without these results, of course. Simply setting your sights on big goals gets you nowhere with the media, or anyone else. You must accomplish them.

The lesson for the rest of us is to persevere. Don't give up. Keep pushing. But, also work smart and be continually looking for new ways to solve the big problem you have committed to solving.

He is outspoken and speaks boldly

As we noted in the opening paragraph of this article, Musk has been known to say outlandish, even cringeworthy, things. In fact, he spouts off unconventional, even crazy-sounding stuff all the time. He often appears to be completely spontaneous and unfiltered. It is part of his persona. And he fired his PR department, so there is no one to rein him in. (*See chapter "Tesla Does Not Have a PR Department. Is That OK?"*)

He also has deeply-held, unconventional, controversial beliefs that he regularly espouses publicly — like bringing Trump back to Twitter, calling out California for its COVID restrictions, threating to fire Tesla and Twitter employees who refuse to come back to the office and not speaking against "diversity, equity and inclusion" (DEI) initiatives.

Of course, we mere mortals can't hope to sail against the prevailing winds of opinion as fearlessly as Musk and still make a living, but I think we can learn to simply be honest in the way we speak. Describe situations as we truly see them to clients, employees, the public and the media, and don't say things we don't believe, no matter how attractive it is to join the chorus.

He is quirky

As someone with Asperger's Syndrome, quirkiness is kind of ingrained into Musk. He literally cannot help it. This manifests itself by, for example, attending the Met Gala with his mother, doing a nerdy dance on the Tesla assembly line, walking into Twitter headquarters carrying a sink, smoking a joint on Joe Rogan's show, Tweeting that he would take Tesla private for $420 a share (a marijuana reference) and on and on. Stupid stuff.

It also means he is unafraid to publicly change his mind, which is, of course, the gravest error for normal people on the public stage.

But it is exactly his quirkiness that makes him the world's only loveable billionaire. He comes across as childlike, innocent — basically well-meaning in his unconventionality.

What can an ordinary business owner like us learn from this? Be authentic. Embrace your differences, what sets you apart, even if it does not seem attractive or "right." Don't cultivate affectations, but don't be afraid to be who you are.

So, want to be loved by the media (and perhaps run a better business, as well?) Be like Elon: Think big. Accomplish much. Be honest and outspoken. And embrace the whole you, not just the antiseptic parts.

- Originally appeared in Forbes

PR Lessons from Sailing

Though I was raised hundreds of miles from the sea, I'm fascinated by sailing. I like the freedom — the complete independence from fuel and motors and all artificial means — and the mastery it requires to tame a powerful natural force. It also teaches humility, because wind and waves can kill as well as thrill. (I learned that a capable sailor weathers a storm by moving with a stronger force versus fighting it, for example.)

I also like sailing because the skills and temperament it requires and the challenges and joys it offers are similar to those of my profession.

Sailing uses a freely available natural force, the wind.
PR takes advantage of another freely available natural force —
humankind's natural desire to be "in the know"

Sailing uses a freely available natural force, the wind, to move a boat in a desired direction. PR moves public opinion from one place to another by drafting on another freely available natural force — humankind's natural desire to be "in the know."

In sailing, you harness this natural energy with properly trimmed sails, which allows you to sail faster by sailing almost into the wind (known as sailing close hauled) versus with the wind. The same holds true in PR: the more controversy you harness in advancing your cause, the faster and wider are results generated, because people are more likely to follow a controversial story. That is, the closer you sail to disaster, the more powerful your effort.

Sailing close hauled causes the boat to heel, or tip to one side, which can be unnerving to the novice sailor, leading him to depower the boat by turning away from the wind. This is a mistake. Not only will it turn the boat away from its destination, but it also gives the sailor less control, because a boat can only be controlled if it is moving. Additionally, modern boats are designed to sail most efficiently when heeling, so you are losing both efficiency and effectiveness by taking the safe route. (In addition to having less fun.)

The parallel to PR is obvious: it can be scary at the helm of a controversial, high stakes publicity campaign, but the surest way to lose all that you have gained is to suddenly back down. Then it looks like everything you've done up to that point was disingenuous. You're dead in the water.

Speaking of dead in the water, the danger of sailing close to the wind is that there is a low margin of error. If the wind shifts, you can find yourself sailing directly into the wind or being "in irons" – a charming saying that originated with 18th Century pirates who found themselves in irons, that is, shackles, when they lost the wind with a British Navy frigate upon them.

There is a similar danger of going too far in PR, of not being attuned to the winds of public opinion and finding yourself walking the plank.

Any boat larger than about 30 feet requires a crew. One man can't do it all. There are at least two distinct jobs: steering and trimming the sails, and both must be done in concert, as each affects the other.

The helmsman at the tiller steers the boat, which means he is responsible for two key things: 1) keeping the boat going in the right direction, both vis-à-vis the destination and adjusting to the direction of the wind, and 2) telling the crew when and how to trim the sails. That is, he guides the boat and has an important bearing on how fast and smoothly the boat sails, but the crew captures the energy that powers the boat by properly trimming the sails.

The same in PR: the helmsman of a campaign must be finely attuned to the winds of public opinion, must know how to safely take advantage of these winds without being overpowered by them and must have the complete confidence of his crew. The crew must be adept at wringing every last bit of forward momentum from the energy of public discourse by developing intriguing stories, writing compelling pitches and press releases, and persuasively making their case to journalists – without being so forceful that the boat of PR turns into the wind or, heaven forbid, capsizes because journalists think you are a fool.

In sailing, it is usually impossible to arrive at your destination by steering a steady course because it is rare that the winds will always be going in the direction you wish to travel. So, you have to jig-jag your way there, traveling slightly left of your destination, then right, then left and back again. This jigging and jagging is called tacking or jibing. And you'd rather tack than jibe, because you jibe when the wind is behind you, so the force of the wind is greater, thus the greater likelihood of catastrophe.

Similarly, accomplishing a PR goal is typically done indirectly. It is quite unlikely that the journalistic universe is going to line up and consistently deliver exactly the message you want every time, or anytime. You must tack and jibe to get there by developing messages that tangentially advance your message and are newsworthy, and it is safer to work against the headwinds of public opinion than to work with them, because when a strong wind is behind you, it can turn violently against you.

Happy sailing.

Why Working at a Great PR & Marketing Agency Is the Most Fun You Can Have With Your Clothes On

You can make things happen

I began my career as a newspaperman, which is also a heap of fun. After all, what is not to like about spending your day talking with people and writing about what you learn? But journalism is a different kind of fun, like the difference between watching a sport and playing it. That is, as a reporter I wrote about what other people did. I was not an instigator. As a public relations consultant and marketer, I make things happen, and that is much more fun. I still spend most of my day talking with people and writing about it. The difference is, I now talk about what our agency and clients accomplish, and I write to make it happen.

> *It's not a life for everyone, but if it's the life for you,
> then PR/marketing agency work is the
> purest blend of work and pleasure.*

You can enjoy stress

There is a fair amount of stress in a PR/marketing agency because we need to get a lot done in a brief time with a few smart people. Of course, stress is your brain telling you it's running in overdrive. And that can be a lot of fun — all your senses are on high alert, time moves at blazing speed, everything you do is intentional, adrenaline is pumping. Of course, to be energized by stress instead of frozen by it, you must be the kind of person who would rather wear out than rust out. It's not a life for everyone, but if it's the life for you, then PR/marketing agency work is the purest blend of work and pleasure.

Another word for stress in the good sense is "flow," a concept described by writer Mihály Csíkszentmihályi as "the mental state of operation in which a person performing an activity is fully immersed in a feeling of energized focus, full involvement, and enjoyment in the process of the activity."

You can use your education

How many people do you know whose jobs have little to nothing to do with the college degree they earned? Many, I am sure, perhaps most. Humanities majors, in particular, tend to suffer this indignity, with English majors running muffler shops. It is becoming such a problem that liberal arts colleges like my alma mater, Centre College, are going out of their way to emphasize the success of their graduates in the workforce. Some are even adding vocational majors, like business and communications. (Yes, even Olde Centre now has a business major.)

I'm an English and philosophy major who uses his education every day. No other education could have better prepared me to think clearly and communicate persuasively — what I am paid to do. What other career, especially in business, rewards knowledge of literature and ideas?

You can work with smart people

We spend at least one third of our waking life at work. Those hours are a lot more interesting if the people you spend them with are fully alert, well-educated, confident and sharp — as are people who staff a great PR and marketing agency.

To me, this is the main benefit of working in a marketing agency — you are surrounded by smart people all day, so communication flows more easily, a sense of humor pervades, learning is always taking place and drama is low. Can you think of a better place to work?

Marketing

The average American is exposed to 4,000 to 10,000 marketing messages every day, but notices less than 100 of them.

This section is about how to get noticed. Accordingly, it's the most "how to" section in the book. You'll learn how to write a marketing plan (and why you need one), how to choose media to meet specific needs and other basics of the craft, along with lots of specific tips.

On the other hand, you'll also find quite a bit in this section about the psychological and philosophical foundation of marketing, knowledge that can be helpful in creating marketing programs that change minds, not just shopping habits.

How To Write a Marketing Plan

Here is a step-by-step roadmap for writing a marketing plan.

Research

It's important to know what people think about your company, so spend some time talking to employees, customers, shareholders and community members — anyone who is touched by your company.

> *It is possible to market without a plan*
> *— it is just not likely to be effective.*

Probe to find out what they truly think and how they feel about the company. This cache of valuable information will form the basis for the SWOT analysis portion of your marketing plan.

Competitive analysis

During your research, be sure to ask people who they think your competitors are, and how your company stacks up against them. Then, to learn more, conduct secondary research by reviewing competitors' websites and reviewing news coverage, reviews, social posts and blogs about or by them. Then, using a website like Semrush, Ahrefs or Spyfu, find out how well their websites perform: which keywords they rank for, how many visitors they attract per month, what their authority score is, etc. Throughout this research, look for ways in which your company is similar to and different from competitors. Rank competitors from most to least competitive.

SWOT analysis

You can't get where you want to go if you don't know where you are. That's why you want to start writing your marketing plan with an analysis of your internal situation (your company's Strengths and Weaknesses) and the external situation in which you operate (the Opportunities and Threats in the marketplace). Mine the research you conducted, as well as your own insights, for this information. Be brutally honest. This is the basis for your entire marketing plan, so if you lie to yourself here, your marketing plan will be ineffective.

Goals

The goals section of your marketing plan clearly lays out how you want your business to be different after the marketing plan has been carried out. Make sure they are SMART goals — specific, measurable, attainable, relevant and time-bound — so you'll be able to know whether they were met. For example, a SMART goal would be: "Increase annual sales by 10% by the end of the year."

Objectives

Objectives are the milestones you must hit to achieve your goals. Unlike goals, which are strategic — meaning that they bear directly on the success of your company — objectives are more tactical and generally pertain to the success of marketing activities. For example, an objective might be: "To reach 5,000 sales prospects with an email campaign that has an open rate of at least 30% and a click-through rate of 5%."

Target markets

In this section of the plan, specify whom you intend to reach through your marketing efforts. Generally, this is your customers and prospective customers, but it could also be employees and prospective employees, if the goal is to find qualified job candidates, or government and community leaders, if you are seeking to deal with burdensome regulations or disgruntled factions of the community.

Message

The message is what you want members of the target markets to know about your company in order to cause the behaviour you are seeking, such as buying your product. The message is often some form of the company's unique selling proposition, or USP, which states the unique benefits your company offers and thus the reason for doing business with you instead of your competitors.

Tactics

Tactics — what you will do and how you will do it — are the heart of a marketing plan.

Here's a fairly exhaustive list of marketing tactics:

- advertising: television, radio, print, outdoor and the many types of digital advertising, such as search advertising, display ads, programmatic ads, affiliate marketing, remarketing
- awards and professional recognition
- blogging
- case studies and white papers
- collateral such as brochures, flyers, sales sheets, etc.
- direct mail
- email marketing
- events including parties, seminars and panel discussions, and product and service announcements
- inbound marketing
- influencer marketing
- infographics
- logo and branding
- native advertising and advertorials
- podcasts
- promotions and contests
- publicity
- search engine optimization
- social media
- speaking engagements
- specialty advertising and swag
- strategic partnerships
- surveys
- telemarketing
- trade shows, conferences and conventions
- videos
- webinars
- websites and landing pages
- word-of-mouth marketing

The key is selecting tactics that are most appropriate for your business and the goals you want to achieve. This generally requires the assistance of an experienced marketing professional.

Timeline

A month-by-month timeline for when each tactic will be deployed and for how long, and which tactics will run simultaneously to enhance their overall effectiveness, i.e., a Gantt chart.

Budget

In the budget section of your marketing plan, delineate how much money you will allocate for each marketing tactic.

It is possible to market without a plan — it is just not likely to be effective. Unfortunately, the marketing efforts of many small businesses seem to be largely the result of sales efforts by advertising salespeople, with business owners buying whatever they think is the best deal proffered by local media. These totally unplanned, uncoordinated efforts can produce sporadic results, but usually not sustained growth. Use your marketing dollars wisely: create a plan and stick to it.

- Originally appeared in Forbes

How To Choose the Right Media for Your Message

For communication to occur, someone must create and transmit a message, and someone must receive it. That's fairly obvious. However, people often forget that messages must be transmitted through a medium and that the medium has an effect on the message.

In this chapter, we'll explore the four primary types of media — paid, earned, shared and owned (plus a fifth hybrid category) — and their effects on messages.

Paid media

Paid media, more commonly known as advertising, involves a simple transaction — you pay the media outlet and they transmit your message.

Advantages: You (mostly) have complete control over the message. The only thing you can't do is outright lie — though puffery is allowed. (Puffery is making general claims that can't be proven, such as: "Our product is the best!")

> *People often forget that messages must be transmitted through a medium and that the medium affects the message.*

You can also control when and how your message is shown (such as during a television show that airs at 8 p.m. every Tuesday) and to whom it is shown (such as to married people with children and a household income of more than $100,000).

Disadvantages: Messages delivered via this method are among the least likely to be believed. Because recipients know you tightly control what is communicated through paid media, they also know they are probably not getting the whole story. Now, the degree to which this disadvantage is in play depends on the education and sophistication of your audience, with less-educated recipients more likely to believe what is communicated without reservation.

Advertorials

A hybrid subcategory between paid and earned media, advertorials —
also known by the recently coined, less-pejorative "native advertising"
— are paid media that look like earned media.

Advantages: To some extent, advertorials combine the advantages of
paid and earned media. That is, you can mostly control the content
(there is usually some editing), it somewhat looks like editorial
content (thus has a conditional third-party endorsement) and your
payment guarantees it runs.

The effectiveness of an advertorial depends on the authority of the
media outlet in which it is presented. For example, *Time* magazine is a
strong, legitimate brand, so running an advertorial in *Time* could be
worth what you pay for it. However, there are many "news outlets"
that publish nothing but advertorials and thus have zero credibility.

Disadvantages: Advertorials can be the worst type of media because the
whole premise — running ads that look like an editorial product — is
somewhat dishonest. For this reason, running an advertorial could do
more harm than good. This is why, in general, we advise our clients to
steer clear of this type of "pay to play" media — unless, as is the case
with *Time*, the sponsoring media is impeccable.

Earned media

Earned media, more commonly known as publicity or public
relations, requires you to convince a gatekeeper at a media outlet,
such as an editor or news director, to communicate your message.
Usually, this means your message is communicated indirectly, through
the words of a journalist.

Advantages: A message communicated via earned media is quite
believable because it carries an implied third-party endorsement. That
is, the recipient knows your message had to pass through several filters
to get to them. First, a reporter had to be convinced that your story
was worth telling. Then, the reporter — not you — told the story. And
it had to go through at least one round of editing and fact-checking.

Sometimes, earned media also offers the benefits of paid media in the form of a bylined column, in which case your words are transmitted through a news media outlet with no changes and marked as coming directly from you. Because a bylined column is presented as an "editorial" product, it is seen as more believable than an advertisement — and it generally is, because someone at the media outlet had to agree to run your column. It is not as believable as an article written by a reporter, however, because it came directly from you, and so is colored by your perception of the issue.

Disadvantages: Earned media is hard to do because you must convince a journalist to tell your story. It's not just writing a check. It takes skill and experience.

Aside from bylined columns (which are less believable, though still more believable than ads), you have little control over the message. Ultimately, the journalist who interviews you decides what to write. Now, this is a reasonable risk to take if you know what you are doing. In my 35+ years in the public relations profession, there have maybe been one to two instances when our work to place a story with a journalist has resulted in negative coverage.

Shared media

Shared media is social media, where a community of people shares content with each other — and where ownership of the content is shared with the owner of the social channel, who can choose to censor your message.

Advantages: In many ways, and a key to its effectiveness, social media is an electronic version of word-of-mouth marketing, and thus has the advantage of using a community as the source of information. It is more immediate and more tailored to our interests than other media, thus more relevant and believable. (I became one of the first proponents of LinkedIn for these reasons.) Interactivity makes it compelling; speaking back to a media draws us in.

Disadvantages: Like word-of-mouth, mistakes, bad news, gaffes and other snafus on social media are amplified quickly and loudly — much more so than good news. Effective social media marketing requires a skilled hand at the tiller.

Owned media

Owned media is the kind of media — such as blog and podcasts — in which you or your organization creates all the content communicated.

Advantages: Because you own it, you have complete control over what is communicated, and it costs you nothing (except for the cost of creating the content, if you hire that out).

Disadvantages: Because the message is coming directly from you with no filter, messages through owned media are less believable than earned media. But the real disadvantage is the size of your audience. Unless you are a national celebrity or are exceptionally effective at creating compelling content, the reach of owned media is likely to be much smaller than that of other types of media.

Each of the several types of media has its use if you know how to use them, which is why it is important to focus as much on the medium as the message in designing your marketing program.

- Originally appeared in Forbes

How a Marketing Partnership Can Energize Your Brand

One of our clients pulled off one of the most creative and effective marketing partnerships I've ever seen — and they did it only a few weeks after the company was founded. (The founder later sold the business to a Fortune 100 company for a handsome sum — his third business exit — about eight years after starting the company.)

Roadie is an "on the way" delivery company that gives ordinary folks a chance to make a little money by delivering items to places that are on the way to where the driver is already traveling. When the company opened, its main need was to recruit drivers. Thanks its partnership with the Waffle House restaurant chain, Roadie soon had all the drivers it needed.

> *Brand partnerships can offer benefits*
> *that are hard to get any other way.*

The partnership was simple: Waffle House restaurants became "Roadie Roadhouses," where drivers and senders connected to hand off or pick up items to be delivered. The restaurants advertised the partnership with in-store signage and offered a free waffle and drink to drivers picking up deliveries at their store.

Waffle House benefitted by driving traffic to its restaurants, as well as associating a very established brand with the hipness of a tech startup. Roadie got to advertise its company to potential drivers across 25 states at virtually no cost — and both benefitted from the publicity generated by the unusual partnership, which exploded when Jimmy Kimmel talked about it during his ABC talk show. Kimmel's best line was a quote from Roadie CEO Marc Gorlin, who said he partnered with Waffle House because, in the South, "you can't throw a dead cat without hitting one."

What are the keys to a successful brand partnership? I suggest there are three:

Brands should be similar but different

The two brands partnering need to have similar values and appeal to a similar audience, but they must be different enough for the partnership to be interesting and attract attention.

For example, BMW and Louis Vuitton are selling a similar experience, luxury travel, to the same market, wealthy individuals with a sense of style. This partnership was not an event, but a product: Louis Vuitton created a four-piece luggage set that fits like a glove into the trunk of BMW's all-electric BMW i8. The partnership was part of the launch of the i8.

The partnership should be newsworthy

What two brands decide to do together should be unusual enough to capture the media's attention.

Star Wars and CoverGirl offer a splendid example. Talk about an odd pairing — what could a science-fiction movie and a makeup company possibly have in common? Well, decades ago, when the *Star Wars* franchise began, probably nothing, because the movie attracted mainly men and boys in the beginning. But today, the old gender and age categories no longer apply — women and girls like *Star Wars*, too. To tap into this new reality, CoverGirl designed a new line of makeup with two styles: the "light side" and the "dark side." The unusual promotion helped put *Star Wars* in front of a demographic it needed more of — females — and allowed CoverGirl to ride the *Star Wars* marketing machine.

Sometimes, the newsworthiness isn't in how different the two brands are, but in what they decide to do together. Both GoPro and Red Bull are lifestyle brands that are all about an action-packed and usually extreme lifestyle. They have been involved in many mutually beneficial partnerships, but the biggest and most spectacular was Stratos, an event they jointly sponsored in which Austrian skydiver Felix Baumgartner jumped from space — 24 miles above the surface of the Earth — with a GoPro camera strapped on. Baumgartner set multiple world records and generated huge press for GoPro and Red Bull that bolstered their "extreme living" brands.

There must be benefit parity

Both brands should receive about the same level of benefit. One should not benefit disproportionately, and one certainly should not benefit at the expense of the other.

For example, part of Starbucks' ambiance is the music played in its coffee shops, and people who buy expensive coffee are pretty good prospects to buy new music. In this partnership, Spotify lets Starbucks baristas use its premium subscription service at no charge. Starbucks gets free access to the latest music and Spotify's artists get access to Starbucks' customers, who can tap into the daily playlists through the Starbucks Mobile App.

Brand partnerships can offer benefits that are hard to get any other way — like lots of attention for a relatively small spend, the opportunity to draft off each other's brand equity and new energy to brands that may have grown a bit long in the tooth. If your company can use these kinds of results, look around for a good partner, come up with an innovative idea and go for it.

- *Originally appeared in Forbes*

How To Create a Company Anniversary People Will Love

Too often, when planning a company anniversary, people get caught up in "stuff" like logos and merchandise and parties and websites and everything but what is really important – and they end up wasting a lot of money with not much to show. No one is really affected. Nobody's feelings about the company change. Nothing is much different than before.

Focus on what is important – the people
who made the company great
and the story of their journey.

To create a successful business anniversary, focus on what is important – the people who made the company great and the story of their journey. Here is a six-step process to make this happen:

Decide why you want to celebrate your anniversary

Simply reaching a significant number of years in business – 10, 20, 25 years – is alone not a valid reason to celebrate a company anniversary. I mean, you can have a celebration, and many businesses do, but you may end up wasting a lot of time and money if you don't have a good reason for celebrating.

First, decide what you want the anniversary to accomplish. It might be to help you enter a new market or launch a new product, or deal with increased competition, or raise the profile of your CEO. There are many good reasons to celebrate an anniversary. Just make sure you have one, and then build your celebration around it.

Have a champion

Celebrating an anniversary right is a big undertaking and you need a person in-charge who is excited about it, understands why it is being celebrated and has the authority to make things happen (or has the complete backing of someone with that level of authority). This person must be organized and capable of motivating people. And having a sense of humor is a definite plus.

It is the job of this anniversary champion to:

- Organize and run a committee that will create the celebration.

- Assign tasks and assure they are carried out.

- Set a budget and track expenses against it.

- Be the liaison between the company and all outside parties pertaining to anniversary matters.

- Keep the entire company apprised about anniversary activities.

- Generate enthusiasm for participating in anniversary activities.

This is not usually a full-time job, but it is a big job. So be sure your anniversary champion can devote at least one-quarter of his or her time to this, which will probably mean shifting some work off your champion for the four to six months it will take to plan and execute your celebration.

Commit the resources necessary to succeed — including CEO buy-in

The first job of the champion is to do a back-of-the-envelope budget for the entire shebang and get approval to spend that amount — or to adjust the budget to an approved level. The champion should also set a minimum budget below which a celebration will not be possible.

Budget approval is one of two absolutes to the success of an anniversary celebration. The other is the total and enthusiastic support of the CEO. Make sure he or she is clear on this, and that everyone in the company understands that this is a top priority for the leader. If you don't have this, your anniversary celebration will eventually be shunted aside when "real" work must be done.

Tell the story

Every company has a story and a storyteller. The story is the lore, maybe even somewhat mythical, about how the company started and where it is going. It's the early struggles, the milestone successes, the heartbreaking setbacks, the eventual triumph and the bright future. And there is usually one person, maybe two, who knows the story better than anyone else — someone who embodies the story. Of course, everybody usually knows who this is, so they won't be hard to find.

Engage your storyteller. Get them to tell the story — the big story and all the little stories it is composed of. This won't all come out at once. It will take a while. Stop by their office every week or so and ask them to tell you again about that time that somebody did something and something happened. It will inevitably lead to more stories, so keep digging. Gather a group of employees occasionally at the end of the day to talk about the old days with your storyteller. Having a bunch of people around often encourages them to open up. And a little wine might be a good idea.

After you've gathered the story, write it up in a way that conveys its almost mythical meaning. And be sure it has an overarching theme, a big idea that inspires people. Then chop it up into bitesize chunks that are easy to tell and that can be categorized so that you can weave the story into almost any situation.

Then, weave the story into the reason for your anniversary, so that everything ties together — and so your reason is authentic to the company and its history, not just something tacked on.

Unearthing, composing and telling your company story will be the most difficult part of this entire process — maybe one of the most difficult things you will ever do — yet also the most important. Having a compelling story is what sets a great company apart from others. (A *great story is behind the success of great countries, too. See chapter "Lessons from the Roman Empire."*)

Make it about people, not stuff

Too often, company anniversaries are about stuff, like gifts emblazoned with the anniversary logo, or a special anniversary website, or an incredible party with amazing food or myriad other thing. These things are fine and good, and they can certainly help you create a memorable celebration, but they are not what the anniversary is about. An anniversary is about people.

Make sure that every important aspect of your anniversary involves identifying and celebrating the people who made it possible for the company to survive and thrive for so many years. This is more than the people who work there. Broaden your reach to involve as many people as possible – customers, investors, reporters who cover the company, alumni, spouses, children, vendors, suppliers, maybe even competitors. Go beyond simply inviting these people to lifting them up, showing the role they played in making the company successful, and thanking them.

Do one memorable thing

Focus all your energy on doing one thing that people will remember for the rest of their lives. *(Like the party at a country music star's home described in the next chapter.)* Spend about one-third of your time, energy and money on this one thing. I can't tell you what it is. It is unique to your company. Be thinking about it throughout this entire process. Sleep on it. It will come to you if you work hard enough and believe it will happen.

I've not provided a handy list of company anniversary ideas you can turn into a checklist and work your way through – because a successful anniversary is not the product of a checklist. It is the result of love. Follow the process outlined here and you may find yourself falling in love with your company and the people who made it, and from that will emerge an anniversary truly worth celebrating.

- Originally appeared in Forbes

How To Throw a Party People Will Talk About for the Rest of Their Lives

We once helped a client plan and throw an incredible 15th anniversary party at the home of country music star John Rich. Thanks to thoughtful planning, meticulous execution, a unique location, a marvelously gracious host and plain old star power, it was one of those once-in-a-lifetime occasions that people tell their grandchildren about.

> *I learned from John Rich how to*
> *throw an event that people are clawing to get into*
> *and don't want to leave.*

Of course, there are many well-planned, well-organized events. What set this anniversary party apart was John Rich. Here are the lessons I learned from Rich about how to throw an event that people are clawing to get into and don't want to leave:

Don't do it if you don't feel it

Rich is not just an artist, he is also a professional with a finely tuned business sense, so he doesn't invite strangers into his home for a huge party just because it would be a blast. It was a business transaction.

By the same token, there are easier ways for a big-time recording artist to make a buck. For that reason, he does not regularly host business events at his home, though he has been known to host fundraisers for non-profits he endorses.

So, did we just get lucky when we approached him about having our client's anniversary party at his home? Maybe. I'm not sure. But what I do know is that Rich felt a strong connection to our client's company and its entrepreneurial journey over its first 15 years. In some ways, it was similar to his own journey of combining hard work, perseverance and native smarts to create a life's work. As he made clear every step of the way in planning and carrying out this event — including his congratulatory remarks from the stage during the party — he really understood the culture of the client company, and the journey of its leaders. He didn't have to manufacture enthusiasm.

Help with promotion

Rich was happy to help us promote the party to our client's clients and prospects across the country. (We held the party during a national industry conference in Nashville so that important people from across the nation would be in town.) For example, he spent an afternoon with us to film a video invitation – picking up his guitar at one point to sing part of it. He even allowed us to incorporate the music and images from one of his music videos. You can imagine how much more powerful a video invitation featuring a big star is than an ordinary mailed or emailed invitation. A serious buzz began in the client's industry when these video invitations started going out.

Focus on what it's worth, not what it costs

A super event like this is not a cheap date. Was it worth it to our client? Absolutely. In terms of new business generated from both existing and new clients, it was worth every penny, and more. John Rich was smart enough to know that value is a function of results, not costs – and he knew he could deliver the results.

Don't nickel and dime

For a set fee, we got everything – all drinks and food, wait staff and bartenders, a professional photographer, security, an event coordinator, Rich's performance – plus the star's commitment to mix with the crowd throughout the night and pose for as many photos with guests as they wanted. He even opened his personal cigar humidor to the party guests. Every possible facet of the event was included so there was no need to, or even possibility of, niggling over details. As a result, things went very smoothly, no nerves were frayed and everyone stayed friends at the end.

Surprise and delight

Our agreement was that Rich would perform a 45- to 60-minute acoustic set during the party. That is, just him and his guitar, which would have been wonderful and more than enough to make partygoers feel special. But, a few days before the event, Rich told us that he was going to bring his full band at no extra charge just because he wanted our client to have a spectacular event. The performance, which lasted well past 60 minutes — I mean, it was a real concert in an intimate setting, just incredible — blew people away. Rich and his band put their heart and soul into it, nothing perfunctory. The room was engulfed by the energy of a man and his band who obviously love what they do.

Of course, not everyone can afford a party at a country music star's home, so what lessons can we glean from this once-in-a-lifetime event? I suggest it is to realize that not every event is once-in-a-lifetime, but when such an opportunity comes along, you need to reach for the stars — spend a little more money than you are comfortable with, pour your heart and soul into it, expect everyone involved to bring their A Game (and find others to work with if they don't) and seek to surprise and delight by providing your guests with unexpected experiences.

How To Harness Word-of-Mouth

When it comes to marketing, nothing beats word-of-mouth.

What makes word-of-mouth effective is the perception that it is difficult to manipulate it. You believe your friend is telling you the absolute truth about the latest product he bought or service he employed — because he is.

Find influential people and
tell them things no one else knows.

However, it is possible to harness the power of word-of-mouth to meet a marketing objective. It's a matter of knowing the right people, treating them right and having the right message.

The right people

The right people are "Influentials" — individuals who have a lot of acquaintances, though not necessarily close friends, across several networks. I'm not talking about social media Influencers (though they can be part of the network), but people who are well-known in "real life" across many different circles, such as within their church, profession, club and political party. They are also more involved in civic affairs than the average person — tending to write letters to the editor and to elected officials, to serve on non-profit boards, to attend political rallies and so forth. Unsurprisingly, they are typically in leadership positions. *(See chapter "Some People Matter More Than Others" for more about Influentials.)*

Treating them right

Treating influential people right means treating them like the important people they are, with respect, deference and courtesy. One way to do this is by telling them something important that no one else knows — and assuring them that they will always be the first to know about important developments at your company or organization. This not only makes Influentials feel good about themselves (and you), but also makes it likely that they will pass on the message you've shared, because people love passing on "inside" information. Doing so is a source of power and prestige, which influential people particularly value.

The right message

If the message you give your network of Influentials is not interesting, even exciting, it won't be passed on. For example, say you are a bank that has created an advisory board of influential people and you announce to the group, which comprises primarily small business owners, that the bank is coming out with a new concierge service for small business owners who maintain a minimum average monthly balance of $100,000. This service aids in booking travel, childcare, shopping, auto maintenance — just about anything a business owner would like to get off his plate. This is a big, exciting message that has high relevance to the small business owners who make up the advisory board, and you can bet it will be passed on. Whereas telling them about a new ATM installation is not news they would share.

How word-of-mouth built a symphony hall

We once put these tactics to work to generate broad, citywide support for a new symphony hall in Nashville. The problem we were charged with solving was the perception in the community that building a new symphony hall was an elitist endeavor — and therefore not worthy of broad community support.

We addressed this problem by creating a 400-member organization of the most influential people in town across all sectors of the community, naming it the Nashville Advisory Council. We created this council by identifying two key community leaders in 15 different sectors — such as religion, business, arts, real estate, nonprofits and entertainment — and asking them to recruit 10-12 other leaders like themselves. And we made it easy to recruit members by making the requirements of membership very non-taxing — which was simply to attend two events a year, during which members would be the first in town to hear about the latest developments in the symphony center project.

At these semi-annual events, Council members were the first to see the plans for the hall, the first to sit in the several types of seats architects were evaluating, the first to see the interior design, the first to hear about the hall's acoustical refinements. They were given VIP hardhat tours of the construction site and engraved metal membership cards that looked like prestigious American Express "Centurion Black Cards." They were the only people invited to sign a massive concrete panel just before it was installed on the roof. (You can still see their signatures in the symphony hall's attic.) Between these events, we kept council members apprised of symphony hall developments via an email newsletter distributed only to them.

It worked. We had 400+ influential Nashvillians spreading the word throughout all sectors of the community about the many benefits a world-class concert hall would bring to the city — such as economic development, education, downtown revitalization, international renown for our city, as well as an amazing concert experience for all kinds of music, not just classical, a venue worthy of a city known for its music. The message was that everyone would benefit from the new hall, even if they never attended a concert there, because of the many benefits it would bring to the city as a whole. And the message had credibility, and legs, because it was transmitted by the city's most influential people.

- Originally appeared in Forbes

How To Market to Old Money

If you do business with the beneficiaries of multi-generational wealth, i.e., Old Money, you realize that Scott Fitzgerald was on to something. The rich *are* different than you and I.

Old Money is a special kind of wealth. It describes more a social class than an economic one. Getting the attention of someone in this class requires something special.

> *Old Money is not looking to find*
> *a new and better way because, frankly,*
> *it has already found it, thank you very much.*

Though I have been around Old Money a bit in my life, I am certainly not from Old Money, so I can't share insider knowledge. But I can share the observations of someone who was to the manor born and authored a book about it, Nelson W. Aldrich Jr. whose great-grandfather – the first Nelson Aldrich – made a fortune in the late 19th Century as a US Senator. (Using the privileges and the patronage of political office, especially the US Senate, has long been a road to immense wealth, sadly.)

In his book, *Old Money, the Mythology of America's Upper Class*, Aldrich describes what Old Money is, what it isn't and how to navigate this somewhat unreal world. The first rule of Old Money is: Don't talk about money, especially the making of money. The main advantage of multi-generational wealth, Aldrich says, is it allows one to opt out of the rat race of making a living and instead focus on making a life, one that is true and good and beautiful. Old Money is not interested in your business ideas or in the idea of business itself, with all its grubbiness and impermanence and risk.

Unlike the entrepreneur, or "Market Man," as Aldrich calls him, Old Money does not care about innovation, or bold moves, or continuous improvement, or finding a need and filling it. Old Money cares about what is timeless, ageless, static, secure, safe and approved. It is not looking to find a new and better way because, frankly, it has already found it, thank you very much, and would like to keep things exactly as they are.

The problem with having enough money to do whatever you want and avoid whatever you want — like work — is that one can become soft and weak. Avoiding this fate is the reason Old Money children are frequently sent away to boarding school at a relatively youthful age, where they are challenged to perform at an elevated level and are surrounded by meritocrats, not indulgent family members. This is a very formative time in the life of an heir, leading to experiences that stay with her the rest of her life. Thus, one way you can break through the armor of Old Money is by tying what you are selling to the special atmosphere of prep schools: the comradery, the insouciance, the lofty standards, the assumption that you are special, and so is everyone around you. (Ralph Lauren nailed this, of course.)

Education is high on the list of what Old Money cares about, because the schools and colleges that teach Old Money children are the most important tools for perpetuating Old Money. Prestigious colleges and universities — particularly Ivy League schools — train Old Money how to act like Old Money.

Prestigious schools are also the primary avenue whereby one born outside the Old Money circle can get inside. These schools perform the great service to Old Money of vetting and injecting new talent into the herd so it remains vigorous. This valuable function that esteemed schools play is well known to Old Money, which is why they are held in such high regard, fear even, and this is also why marketing campaigns to Old Money are more likely to succeed if they involve support for (or from) highly selective colleges and universities.

Military adventure is another time-honored way that Old Money toughens up its young, so if your business is involved with or can become involved with military brass (not so much the G.I.s) you are more likely to be taken seriously by Old Money. The military's strict code of honor and adherence to old fashioned values, like valor, and its lack of concern with the marketplace and civilian life, also speak to Old Money.

In day-to-day life, Old Money cares about social graces and social virtues, Aldrich says. Social graces are simply good manners, which is more about making others feel comfortable and respected than it is using the right fork at dinner. Social virtues, the signs of and result of "good breeding," are the old fashioned, timeless values that can seem rather corny because they attest to a belief that there are absolutes in life, that not everything is relative and that some things (and some people) are superior to others. Aristotle's 12 Virtues will serve for an example of the values behind social virtues: courage, temperance (moderation), liberality (not being stingy), magnificence (charisma, style), ambition, patience, friendliness, truthfulness, wit (humor, joy), modesty, and justice. Tie your product or service to these values and, if your prey is Old Money, you are more likely to succeed.

So, to sum up, if you seek to do business with Old Money, don't talk about business, embrace lifelong learning and immerse yourself in timeless values. Even if you don't make a dime off them, you may live a more satisfying life by emulating the ways of America's homegrown aristocracy.

How To Market To Dirty Harry

I recently re-watched the movie *Dirty Harry* and everything became clear to me — as clear as everything is to Harry Callahan. Never wavering and always sneering at less worthy beings, Inspector Callahan is never unsure about anything — other than whether he shot five or six times in the excitement of a gun fight. (I am referring, of course, to the famous scene in the movie in which Harry points his .44 Magnum, "the most powerful handgun in the world," at a wounded criminal who is reaching for his gun after a shootout. Harry says he is unsure whether there is a bullet left in his gun, asking the criminal, "Do ya feel lucky, punk?")

Seeing the rock-hard, comic consistency of Clint Eastwood's character and realizing that it is foundational to the movie, I also realized that Harry Callahan is an American archetype and, therefore, a market segment.

"Do ya feel lucky, punk?"

To someone who is a member of the Dirty Harry market segment, things are pretty clear-cut. He knows right from wrong, up from down, in from out and when he sees a problem, he's on it. He's a man of action, or at least that's how he sees himself. And he thinks he is pretty street smart, able to read people well and size up a situation. He doesn't have a big ego (or so he thinks) and although he's not a big church-goer, he generally stands up for values like kindness, honesty and personal responsibility.

The Dirty Harry archetype describes a segment of the American market, and it's likely that the people who comprise this vast swath are key customers for several companies. Boats, Jeeps, beer and pizza come to mind, for starters.

Clear values

The Dirty Harry archetype exhibits values that are clear, consistently stated and quickly acted upon. Harry instinctively knows who the bad guy is (just as he quickly smells out a poseur in the police department or a loser on the street), and he is clear about why they deserve the hell he is about to deal. And justice is swift. When Dirty Harry gets you in his sights, he does not hesitate.

Lesson: To connect your product or service with someone who exhibits this attribute, present a clearly defined, easy-to-see benefit. There are no grays to Dirty Harry. Boldly state the benefits you offer without artifice or embellishment. For instance, put enormous tires on an off-road Jeep. Or provide clearly labeled calorie content on light beer.

A Ulysses-like guile & bravery without bravado

A second Dirty Harry attribute is Ulysses-like guile. Behind the hard-edged, stoic exterior is an agile mind that can quickly turn the tables on a bad guy. And Harry always wins because he doesn't care if he loses; he is flippantly indifferent to everyone and everything.

A third Dirty Harry attribute is bravery without bravado. Harry never showed off when he was shooting it out with a bad guy. It was just business that had to be done, like taking out the trash.

Lesson: To connect with these two attributes, don't try too hard to be noticed. This is a hard one, of course. Getting noticed is the essence of marketing. The key is to be obvious but not overly flashy. The packaging on your frozen pizza box can be really plain if it stands out from the glare of the competition's packaging, for example.

Nontraditional honor & corniness

A fourth Dirty Harry attribute is nontraditional honor. You would never find Harry in a social register or decked out with medals, but you'll also never find him shirking responsibility or using good people wrongly. He honors age-old standards of conduct.

A fifth Dirty Harry attribute is being corny and unsubtle. Any movie that is at least 50 years old, as *Dirty Harry* is, is automatically corny to us because we know all the jokes — and some of them really stand out.

Lesson: To connect to these two attributes, be corny and daring.

Weave "mom and dad" or "working at the office" into your marketing. Find ways to subtly work discredited concepts like masculinity or duty and honor into your messaging. Try not to be "with it." For example, in an ad about a sports car, you could mention that it makes late-night trips to the office a whole lot faster — because nobody "with it" works after hours and certainly not in an office.

This is the Dirty Harry playbook. But this approach of personifying a brand as a movie character can work with most brands. Once you've decided on the character, break that character down to his or her fundamental drives and imagine how your product or service could appeal to and satisfy those unique traits.

Is your brand about a great journey like The Wizard of Oz? Or a saga of long service, wisdom and deep family feelings like Gone with the Wind? Or maybe your brand is Han Solo, ready to take on any challenge to save the day. Look for the unique personality of your brand in the movies, and when you find the right character, you'll have a fully fleshed persona upon which you can drape marketing concepts to try on for size.

- Originally appeared in Forbes

Lessons From Austin

I once joined about 130 fellow Nashvillians on a Chamber of Commerce trip to Austin, Texas to learn how a city very much like Nashville has done very well — especially in building a strong tech industry, something I and our PR firm were involved in bringing about in Music City.

Make it easy to learn and easy to live.

I learned a lot during our three action-packed days in Austin, lessons that are valuable not only to city leaders, but also to marketing pros who want to think bigger.

Talent matters more than anything

Austin has succeeded for many reasons, but the main reason is the concentration of talented people who live there. Some of the nation's most innovative businesses are moving to Austin to have access to this incredible talent pool.

How did Austin become a magnet for talent? The city makes it easy to learn, with great public and private universities. It also makes it easy to live, thanks to Texas's low tax philosophy.

Lesson: Encourage your people to be lifelong learners and give them the resources, like a training budget, that enable this to happen. And don't overtax them with small-minded tasks. Make sure they have time to stretch their imagination.

Expect resistance all the time

There is a strong "no growth" contingent in Austin, especially among the political class, which makes economic progress a constant challenge. As a result, business-minded folks in Austin must be both persistent and innovative.

Lesson: Seek out challenging projects and clients to keep you on your toes, and realize that your strongest competitors have the most to teach you.

Play to your competitors' weaknesses

One of Austin's biggest advantages is that it is not in California, New York or Illinois — high-tax states that are shedding talented, productive people. Of the 570 companies that have moved to Austin in recent years, 168 of them are from California.

Lesson: Look for competitors that are making their customers unhappy and show how your company can make them happy.

Don't buy customers

Of the 570 companies that recently moved to Austin, only 18 got any kind of financial incentive — a remarkable track record today, when corporate relocation executives regularly extract huge tax abatements from cities.

Lesson: Don't compete on price. It may get you a few customers, but they won't be loyal and will leave for the first competitor who offers them a better bribe.

Plant seeds for tomorrow's successes

Austin is now in the fourth generation of its tech boom. It is strong today because companies like IBM, Motorola and Texas Instruments established a presence in the city decades ago. They laid the foundation of the culture that today attracts the best and the brightest away from California, New York and Illinois.

Lesson: Build a legacy by deciding to be good at a few things, instead of trying to be OK at everything.

Embrace "coopetition"

There is a collaborative culture in Austin. Competitors believe that a rising tide lifts all boats, so they often work together for the good of the entire economy. They still compete, mind you, but it's not cutthroat and they learn from each other.

Lesson: Get to know your competitors and don't be afraid to get together with them occasionally to share information that can make you both better.

Cross-pollinate

One of the most unique things in Austin is the way that private enterprise and the public sector work together to solve civic problems. This kind of cross-pollination has led to some very innovative solutions, such as a private equity fund that invests in affordable housing projects.

Lesson: Get outside your comfort zone. Seek out people and organizations that can provide you with a radically different viewpoint, and be open enough to learn from them.

- Originally appeared in Forbes

Why Content Marketing?

Content marketing is a relatively new term (some say it was officially coined around 1996), though the concept also has a long history, dating back to Benjamin Franklin's *Poor Richard's Almanack*, in which, to promote his printing business, Franklin published thought-provoking content about everything BUT printing.

Content marketing is providing your prospects and customers with information, usually at no charge, that helps them solve a problem without obviously trying to sell them something. Examples of content marketing include case studies, white papers, eBooks, blogs, videos, infographics, podcasts and checklists. The best content marketing provides information that people would expect to pay for.

It is the only truly authentic form of marketing, because your only motive is to help people, not sell them. The beauty is, when you help them, they sell themselves.

Here are eight reasons why your business should be doing content marketing:

1. Having regularly updated, keyword-focused and properly linked content on your website is key to attracting search engine-generated traffic — because it is providing exactly what a search engine is looking for, i.e., clear, honest and well-communicated answers to questions.

2. Today's customers expect to receive valuable content BEFORE they buy. Without content marketing, you're out of the game. The psychological foundation of this approach is the principal of reciprocity, which holds that people who receive a gift — even a gift they did not want — are hardwired to reciprocate by providing the gift-giver something else of value, that is, by buying what the company behind the content marketing campaign is selling. *(See chapter "The Reciprocity Principle" for more on this topic.)*

3. Consumers want to know who provides the BEST product or service. You become known as the best by providing content that

proves it — like quality tests, customer testimonials, sales figures, case studies, white papers and other proofs of performance.

4. Traditional advertising is losing its effectiveness. Simply "telling" a potential customer that your product or service is the best is no longer believable. You must prove it, which engaging content gives you the bandwidth to do.

5. It takes a long time for content marketing to work — so the sooner you start, the better. Content marketing is about creating an audience with whom you develop a relationship of trust. That doesn't happen overnight. But when it does happen, you are likely to have loyal, evangelistic customers for life.

6. Which brings us to another key benefit of content marketing: it grows a better grade of customer than traditional "push" marketing. A customer acquired through content marketing will stay with you through thick and thin, spend a lot of money over a lifetime, be less likely to shop you and more likely to tell her friends about you. This is because content marketing is focused on identifying and solving a customer's problem, not just selling a product. It is the only form of marketing in which the stuff you create to sell your product — the content you provide — can be almost as valuable as the product itself.

7. You can't be a thought leader without content marketing, and thought leadership is key to owning your market because it establishes you as THE authority on solving a particular problem. Content marketing is fundamental to thought leadership because that's what useful content is — sharing your thoughts. No one ever advertised their way to thought leadership. Lots of people wrote (or videotaped) their way there. (See chapter "How To be a Thought Leader" for more.)

8. Content marketing is simply more fulfilling and fun and honest than most other marketing tactics. Think about it: is it more fulfilling to create an ad or to write a blog post? The former has no purpose other than sales. The latter is about freely sharing lessons learned from solving a particular problem. It is more likely to lead to a conversation than a pitch, that is, it's more about living than

simply earning a living.

So, to sum up: though it is more difficult, more expensive and takes longer than traditional marketing efforts, content marketing is ultimately more effective, more sustainable, more enjoyable and leads to loyal customers, not shoppers. It is also the only truly authentic form of marketing, because your only motive is to help people, not sell them. The beauty is, when you help them, they sell themselves.

- Originally appeared in Forbes

Some People Matter More Than Others

That's right. We are not all the same.

So, what do we do about this fundamental inequality inherent in any population? Well, as marketers, we use it to our advantage, of course. One of the best ways of doing so is finding people who are more influential than others and encouraging them to be part of a word-of-mouth marketing campaign. In fact, word-of-mouth marketing is no more than identifying the most influential people in your target market and convincing them to say complimentary things about you. *(See chapter "How To Harness Word-of-Mouth" for more on this topic.)*

> *Chances are that 1 in 10 of the people you*
> *know are Influentials.*
> *And they matter a lot more than the other 9.*

So, who are these influential people who matter more than others? In the early 21st Century the Roper research organization set out to answer this question in a very precise way. Before we get to their precise answers, let's look at their general findings, which are that influential people:

- *Have an activist approach to life:* That is, they don't just watch things happen or let things happen to them — they make things happen in the community, in the workplace, even during their leisure time.

- *Have a broad network of connections:* Influentials don't necessarily have more close friends than the average person, but they do have considerably more acquaintances — and these "weak connections" are actually more helpful to word-of-mouth efforts than strong ones, because they are better, quicker pipelines for spreading information. Influentials also know people in lots of different networks, rather than a lot of people in a few networks. Most Influentials are connected to seven different groups, versus only three for the typical executive or professional.

- *Have restless minds:* They are easily bored. They love learning and solving problems.

Sound like anybody you know? According to Roper, chances are that 1 in 10 of the people you know are "Influentials." And they matter a lot more than the other 9, at least, they do if your job is to convince the other 9 to do something, like buy a product or vote for a candidate.

Now, as to specifics, Roper's research says that an Influential is someone who has done at least three of the activities on the list below in the past year.

- Attended a public meeting. (75% of Influentials have done this in the past year, which is +58 percentage points above the national average)

- Wrote or called a politician at the state, local or national level. (68%, +56)

- Served on a committee of a local organization. (50%, +43)

- Were officers in a club or organization. (48%, +41)

- Attended a political rally, speech or organized protest. (45%, +38)

- Wrote a letter to the editor or called a live broadcast to express their opinions. (40%, +34)

- Were active members of a group trying to influence public policy or government. (35%, +30)

- Made a speech. (31%, +27)

- Worked for a political party. (25%, +22)

- Wrote an article for a magazine or newspaper. (21%, +18)

- Held or ran for office. (6%, +5)

Now, all these activities have to do with social or political activities. Aren't there influential people who aren't into this kind of stuff? According to Roper, no. But that's not all they are involved in. Roper found that "Influentials stood out from the mainstream not only for being forward-thinking on social and political issues: they brought an activist approach, were engaged in ideas, were attuned to new developments and exercised influence *virtually across the board*." (This quote and all stats in this chapter are from *The Influentials* by Ed Keller and Jon Berry, who were CEO and vice president, respectively of RoperASW, the organization that conducted this research.)

More fun facts about Influentials:

- *They volunteer at about double the rate of the average person and triple the rate of people in higher income households:* This latter fact is key — marketers have traditionally believed that executives, professionals and other high earners account for most influential people. Nope. Although Influentials tend to earn more than others, because they work harder and enjoy their work, a high income alone does not make one an Influential.

- *They are fulfilled by their work:* About 75% of Influentials say they consider their work a career, compared to only 56% of workers overall. They are also 22% more likely to bring work home. And money plays a relatively small role. To 70% of Influentials, the "good life" means having an interesting job, which is 17 points above the percentage of average Americans who say the same thing. And having a lot of money is important to only 46% of Influentials, which is 11 points below the percentage of what most people say.

- *Even their leisure time is active:* They are much less likely to use their leisure time for passive pursuits, like watching sports on TV or watching TV in general. What they most like to do during their time off is read books — 49% of them do this, versus only 27% of the general public. They are also much more likely than the other 90% to do volunteer work on their time off, or travel, or exercise, or play sports, or spend time on hobbies — basically, anything but vegging out in front of the TV.

So, let's say you identify a group of people who are obviously influential. What do you do with them? Two things:

1. Listen. Create an advisory board of Influentials and solicit their opinion on your product or service.

2. Reveal information to them before anyone else. When you come out with a new product or service, show it to your advisory board of Influentials first.

Do these two things and your Influentials will burn up the grapevine with your news.

The Reciprocity Principle

Unsolicited, someone I do not know just mailed me a $50 bill and a letter asking that I accept his phone call.

Will I accept the call? Of course. I don't have a choice.

As Professor Robert Cialdini has proven in his extensive research into the psychology of persuasion, we humans are hard-wired to respond positively to a gift. It doesn't matter whether we want the gift or not, or whether we like or even know the person who gave it to us. We are obligated to repay the favor. The giver, not the recipient, is in the driver's seat. It's the principle of reciprocity.

> *Will I accept the call?*
> *Of course. I don't have a choice.*

The extent of our obligation is proportionate to the size of the gift or favor. If my unsolicited benefactor had mailed me a $1 bill instead of a $50 bill, I might not accept his call, because I think the "3 minutes of my time" he is requesting is worth more than $1. But, $50 is just about right.

It's enough to get my attention and to engage my sense of obligation to repay the unsolicited favor. And, unlike the ubiquitous $20 bill, the $50 is not something we see every day, probably because most of the cash in our wallets comes from ATMs, which do not dispense $50 bills. This makes the $50 special, more likely to grab our attention. And a $100 bill would have been over-the-top, approaching the creepy zone.

Professor Cialdini explains our programmed response to gifts as evolutionary and fundamental to civilization, in that it gives us a reason to cooperate with others by giving us some degree of control over their actions. "We are human because our ancestors learned to share their food and their skills in an honored network of obligation," as famed anthropologist Richard Leakey said. Obligating others to repay the gifts we give them is a way to assure that what we are giving away is not lost to us, because the recipient is obligated at some point in the future to give us a gift in return. So, giving is not a losing proposition, but a winning one. From this perspective, the old adage, "It is better to give than to receive," really means, "It is better to give *because you will receive.*"

So, sending an unsolicited $50 to me was a sound decision psychologically, but was it sound economically? Let's assume that the giver, Milton Milam, EVP of Sales for Benchmark Leadership Training in Chattanooga (a Crestcom International franchise) mailed his packet of testimonials and a $50 bill to 100 people, which would have cost $5,000 for the gift, plus another $500 or so for printing and mailing, or $5,500 total. Then, let's assume that, thanks to the principle of reciprocity, this small direct mailing results in a response rate of 5% instead of the typical 2%. And let's further assume that each engagement with Benchmark Leadership Training, which provides business consulting services, generates a minimum of $5,000 in revenue, which is probably on the low side. Based on these entirely reasonable assumptions, Mr. Milam's $5,500 gift could generate $25,000 in revenue, for an ROI of about 5:1. Even if this effort only results in the typical 2% response rate, Mr. Milam will still just about double his money.

We've achieved similarly spectacular results when putting the principle of reciprocity to work for our clients. For example, several years ago, a client's main marketing challenge was that its sales staff could not get past the receptionist when they called on prospective clients. We solved the problem by sending the prospects a marketing message in a gift. The marketing message was a five-minute video about the client's services, which we loaded onto a new iPod, the gift. We placed the iPod in a specially designed box that displayed the expensive technology to best effect and provided simple, step-by-step instructions for turning on the iPod and watching our video. We placed a company brochure and other printed marketing materials in the box below the die-cut tray that held the iPod. We then gift-wrapped the box and shipped it priority overnight to about 100 prospects.

Receptionists had no choice but to take our gift to their boss — to do otherwise would be theft. Plus, basic human decency dictates that we don't steal others' gifts. Can you imagine not passing on to someone a gift-wrapped package?

Our client had no problem getting through to their prospects from then on. In fact, the program was so successful that we had to stop it. Our client rapidly got more business than they could handle. And it was an economic as well as marketing success. Because our client sold a big-ticket service, closing just one sale easily covered the cost of this very expensive mailing — and they closed a lot more than one.

Some people have built an entire company around the principle of reciprocity, like the guy who literally wrote the book on the subject, entitled *Giftology*. Author John Ruhlin founded a company that sets up and carries out a strategic program of giving gifts to people whom you want to be indebted to you.

Finally, I believe the principle of reciprocity is especially pertinent in the digital sphere. Think about it, most successful digital marketing activities — social media, content marketing, inbound marketing, email marketing — follows the "Give to Get." formula. You never think about asking anyone for anything online until you have first given them something of value, such as a white paper, case study or access to research — that is, valuable, "non-salesy" information. *(See chapter "Why Content Marketing?" for more on this topic.)*

Let "giving before you get" inform your marketing tactics. Mail an unsolicited gift to sales prospects. Surprise outstanding job candidates with a nice piece of company swag. Give employees a gift certificate on their birthday. Step it up a notch by sending gift certificates to their spouse and children on their birthdays — which is a genius gifting idea from my friend Arnie Malham, who authored a best-selling book on creating a great company culture, *Worth Doing Wrong*.

The more you give, the more you get. It's almost a religious experience. Or psychological warfare. Choose your metaphor. The principle of reciprocity may be the most powerful psychological tool in your marketing toolbox.

- Originally appeared in Forbes

Marketing Mythology

Western culture is built on age-old myths, many of them from the ancient Greeks, who created an amazing collection of stories to explain who we are and why we act the way we do. That is, they contain the seeds of modern psychology, which may be why Sigmund Freud and Carl Jung used Greek myths to illustrate the concepts about the mind they explored.

Why does this matter to a marketer? Because creating a brand is fundamentally about tapping into our unconscious to create connections with the brand.

> *Creating a brand is fundamentally about*
> *tapping into our unconscious.*

So, why not go straight to the source? Why not use mythological common knowledge to market a product? That is the inspiration for this chapter, in which we will examine a few Greek myths, find the branding message they illustrate and suggest a likely product or service that could best make use of this mythological approach to marketing.

Prometheus and the theft of fire

The myth: Feeling sorry for humans, for whom the king of gods, Zeus, did not much care, Prometheus stole fire from the blacksmith to the gods and brought it to Earth as gift to humans, who could use it to warm themselves, cook food and make tools — making humans a little more god-like. In retaliation, Zeus chained Prometheus to a rock in the Caucasus Mountains and sent an eagle every day to gnaw out Prometheus's liver, which regenerated each evening, only to be gnawed out again the next day.

The marketing myth: This myth would work well for a brand that wants to be perceived as standing up for the little guy, regardless of the consequences.

Likely industry: The payday loan industry, which provides poor folks with something they need but can't get from "the man" — credit. This industry is also stridently criticized by proper society (the eagle gnawing at the victim's liver) for the work it does.

Theseus and the Minotaur

The myth: Every seven to nine years, Athens was forced to send young people to the island of Crete to be cast into a vast labyrinth and be eaten by the Minotaur, a half-man, half-bull monster. Theseus, the son of the king of Athens, demanded to be part of the next contingent sent to the Minotaur. When he arrived in Crete, the princess of Crete fell in love with Theseus and gave him a ball of thread which he unwound as he walked through the maze, where he found and killed the Minotaur and then followed the unrolled skein of thread to exit the maze.

The marketing myth: Don't lose your way fighting monsters. That is, don't become so focused on solving arcane problems that you forget about the customer's needs today.

Likely industry: Any company in the software business, because it's easy to become enamored with features to the point that the software becomes too complicated to use.

Perseus and the Gorgon Medusa

The myth: Perseus, a demigod (the son of a god and a mortal), sought to kill the monster Medusa, a woman who has snakes for hair and, thus, was so ugly that anyone who looked on her was turned to stone. To protect himself from becoming an instant fossil, Perseus looked indirectly at Meduss (relying on her reflection on his shield) and cut off her head. He then used the severed head to turn his enemies into stone.

The marketing myth: The brand is about seeking novel ways to solve supposedly intractable problems — and about how the lessons learned from solving a difficult problem can give you power.

Likely industry: This would be a great myth for a plaintiff's law firm that finds creative ways to turn horrible actions by the defendants

130

against them.

Orpheus and Eurydice

The myth: Orpheus, who played the lyre, was the greatest musician of
all time. His music could charm even rocks and rivers. One day, he
fell in love with Eurydice, wooing her with his music, of course. But
their love affair was short-lived, for Eurydice was soon bitten by a
poisonous snake and died. Heartbroken, Orpheus traveled to hell to
convince Hades, the king of the underworld, to release his bride —
gaining access to hell by lulling to sleep with his lyre Cerberus, the
three-headed dog that guards the underworld. Hades was also
charmed by Orpheus' music and agreed to let Eurydice follow
Orpheus back to the light, provided Orpheus did not turn to look at
her before they had left hell. However, just as they were about to exit,
Orpheus, thinking he had been tricked by Hades, turned to make
sure Eurydice was behind him, and lost her forever.

The marketing myth: The brand message is "Don't look back until the
journey's done." Keep your head down. Stay focused. Don't be
distracted.

Likely industry: I can see this myth working for a business coaching
firm, which is all about clients trusting the process, doing the work
and sticking with it until results are achieved. Never looking back,
always forward.

Of course, we have just scratched the surface of the treasure of Greek
myths. For a wonderful collection to peruse for your branding
pleasure I suggest you read *Mythology* by Edith Hamilton, the classic re-
telling of the myths that undergird our culture. Read this great
literature with an eye for branding by teasing out the psychological
truths that lie beneath the entertaining stories.

- Originally appeared in Forbes

Marketing Archetypes

Carl Jung created the concept of synchronicity, which is basically meaningful coincidences, like:

- You're thinking about fish.
- On the front page of today's newspaper is a photo of a gigantic fish somebody caught.
- There's a big aquarium at the restaurant where you had lunch.
- And — a month ago — you RSVP'd for a party tonight at a sushi restaurant.

Jung would say, "Hey, something is going on with this fish thing. I wonder what it is?"

He found out and called it an archetype.

Jung was the pioneer of holistic psychology, which espouses the idea that there is a central force, pattern or story connecting the spiritual, emotional and physical worlds. That is, we can interact psychically with the material world, and vice versa. Jung had a word for it: psychoid — the merging of space, time and spirit.

> *It's always easier to latch onto an idea that's already in someone's head than to implant a new one.*

Archetypes are eruptions of the Universal Unconscious, the mysterious lore that is common to all cultures. Nestled in this deep layer of humanity's legacy are timeless concepts like the wise old man, the great mother, the trickster and the hero. Like Zeus, Hera, Hermes and Odysseus. Like Morgan Freeman, Oprah Winfrey, Joaquin Phoenix and Mel Gibson. You get the idea.

Archetypes are the building blocks of our culture, religion and literature. They are the stories that underlie every story.

So, if you think Jung is onto something (and I do), you could design marketing programs that call up and connect with archetypes. That is, tell stories that evoke narratives that already exist in our hearts and minds. It's always easier to latch onto an idea that's already there than it is to implant a new one.

Tell the story

First, find the storyteller in your company. Mine the company's lore for stories about how it started and where it's going. The struggles, the successes, the setbacks, the eventual triumph and the bright future. There is usually one person, maybe two, who knows the story best. And they won't be hard to find because they tell stories to everybody. *(See chapter "How To Create a Company Anniversary People Will Love" for more about capturing your company's story.)*

After you've gathered the story, look to archetypes for story themes, direction and plot. An excellent place to start is Greek mythology, which is packed with ready-made archetypes.

Then, tell your story in a way that evokes your chosen archetypes. Maybe your goal is to establish the CEO as the "wise old man." So you place articles with his byline in national publications. You find opportunities for him to speak to professional and industry groups. You start a regularly scheduled podcast on which he interviews the leading lights of your profession. Need inspiration? Prime your imagination by identifying archetypical wise men in pop culture, like Obi-Wan Kenobi, Fred Rogers, Gandalf or Yoda. Think about what sets them apart, what made people believe in them, respect them. Then find or create stories that emphasize these traits about your leader.

Anthropomorphize organizations

Every organization has a culture and a personality, whether they want one or not. Dig into your culture. Look for stories that verify and expound on the culture. Then think about your company/organization like a person. What kind of hero is your company? Does it provide structure to the world? Then its archetype might be the caregiver/great mother or the king/creator. How does a caring mother or honest and good king act? How do they manifest their power?

For example, if you want to evoke the caring mother archetype, emphasize how your company protects people, just as Volvo — perhaps the ultimate "great mother" company — has long emphasized.

Thinking about marketing through the lens of archetypes is not guaranteed (or even likely) to spark a synchronistic event that amazes customers and dumbfounds competitors. But it might.

What it *is* likely to do is force you to think about your marketing in terms of telling a story. That's worth doing because people like to hear stories, and they especially enjoy listening to stories they already know, that are already part of their own story. It also gives your marketing a strategy, an overall direction and consistency, rather than being a random collection of tactics. In short, thinking mythologically can have very real-world results.

- Originally appeared in Inc magazine

Art in Marketing

We once provided PR and social media services to a shopping and dining complex in a wealthy sub-market of Nashville — The Factory at Franklin. Built in 1929, the former stove factory was repurposed by a local visionary in the 90s into an industrial-chic suburban mall. It's a beloved institution in this stylish small town in one of the fastest growing markets in the country. New owners are investing capital and ideas into reimagining the next era of this landmark.

However, the story is not the real estate development, inspiring though it is. The story is the decision by the developers to hire a fine artist, not commercial artist, to guide the rebrand.

Art can be a perfect mid-term marketing tactic to take over when the afterglow of launch advertising fades.

Working with a pure artist — that is, one whose identity and philosophy are bound up in the art, who sees what he does as a vocation, not an advocation — taught me several lessons about creating a story and keeping it alive via acting it out, not just by laying a marketing grid over it. It also taught me how this merger of art and marketing creates a more meaningful, deeper connection with customers.

To give you an example, I point to a previous project by The Factory at Franklin artist, Bryce McCloud: the launch of the Noelle Hotel in downtown Nashville. Like The Factory at Franklin, the Noelle was an old beauty brought back to life, transformed from an early 20th Century office building into a fashionable boutique hotel.

At the Noelle, McCloud worked with 11 other local artists to come up with a list of iconic, though perhaps overlooked people and places that define Nashville — "an inclusive portrait of the city," as he put it, called "Nashvillians of Note."

Each artist was given a floor — about 8 artworks per floor, hung in the hallway — to display their selection of Nashville icons. This collection of who and what local artists think are Nashvillians of Note included photographs, paintings and drawings of people and places — some well-known, many known only in Nashville, some never heard of before. Walking down the hall of any floor, you would have known it was a themed installation, but you would probably have wondered what the artworks had in common. Going from floor to floor, seeing a distinctive style of art on each, you would have been even more perplexed, perhaps. Certainly curious.

A curious person would want to know more, of course. And McCloud, a letter-press printer, produced a "Nashvillians of Note" catalog, available in the hotel gift shop and elsewhere throughout Nashville, of the entire show — done in the inimitable Nashville letter-press style pioneered by Nashville's Hatch Show Print, but with more clarity and simplicity. That is, more accessible. The catalog is marked "Volume 1" as if promising an annual show, but not really.

And that is the idea, period. As simple, and elegant as that. A lovingly curated experience, tailored to the perspective of a hotel hallway, drawn from the immediate environment and aesthetically matched to the expected recipient — the upscale, educated, curious people traveling in one of the most "authentic" yet ironic cities in the country, Nashville, Tennessee. You'd expect for the gift shop to have something local and interesting, but you don't expect a catalog for a themed, custom art show currently running at the hotel (unless you are staying at 21C Museum Hotel, but even those catalogs pale in comparison to the corny yet ironic "real" Nashville authenticity of the Noelle Hotel catalog).

Though it was an unusual activation of a new brand, this art project was a successful branding experience for the mid-term because: 1) It is dense and multilayered — nearly 100 artworks hung throughout the hotel plus a 150-page book. 2) It is done with obvious artistic skill, thus attracts the of attention of sophisticated customers. 3) And it gives hotel guests something to talk about (and maybe show around) back home.

Part of the Noelle's Hotels' brand story will be this thoughtful art installation. It is a buzz that keeps on buzzing because it will be new to most people staying at the hotel, and they can buy a book or take a selfie and bring it back to share at their home. It is the perfect mid-term marketing tactic to take over when the afterglow of launch advertising fades.

I imagine the Noelle art project was also inexpensive, compared to the cost of a traditional hotel launch campaign. There is certainly nothing high budget about the production.

Now, I said this is a good mid-term marketing tactic. Noelle Hotel did not rely exclusively on an art exhibit and catalog to launch the hotel. The art project was part of an overall launch spend for advertising and social media marketing. It's kind of a truism (though not always true) that if you need an immediate reaction – which you need to launch a new hotel – you need to buy attention ala' advertising.

Paid media leads the way in a launch because there is not enough time for earned media (PR), shared media (social media) or owned media (blogs, art projects, gift catalogs, etc.) – all of which build in effectiveness over time. Only paid media allows you to turn up the volume quickly by simply buying as much time or space as you want (or can afford). But what goes up quickly comes down just as swiftly: advertising is a kind of sugar high that rapidly crests and fades unless you keep adding fuel to the fire.

After the fire of advertising dies away the uniqueness of a tailored artistic performance will keep the embers glowing for several months, that is, mid-term. After that, you could switch out the gallery regularly – as happens at 21C Museum Hotels – or you could just invest in long-term marketing strategies, like website, PR and customer service.

And that is what I learned about marketing from watching an artist do marketing: to let the story (in this case, the untold story of the "real" Nashville) drive the execution.

- Originally appeared in Forbes

Why Literature Matters

I was once a member of two book clubs. One read only literature, the other focused on non-fiction: physics, psychology, history, economics and other dense topics. I managed to convince the non-fiction club to read a novel one time: Hemingway's *The Sun Also Rises*, his first novel — and I think his greatest. (*In Our Time*, a collection of short stories, was his first book, and I think perhaps his greatest book. The strange thing about Hemingway is that he never got any better than his early work. Maybe that's why he eventually blew his brains out.)

Literature teaches the marketer how to use symbols skillfully
to present a believable point of view
that connects with his audience.

The non-fiction book group absolutely hated the Hemingway book. They found nothing redeeming about it at all. Their chief complaint (as far as I can tell, since they hated the book so much they didn't want to talk about it) is that it was about a bunch of characters they did not care about who did nothing but drink, play and bitch at each other. (Drinking being the main motif of *The Sun Also Rises*, as it is in most Hemingway books. No one can make constant drinking seem more natural and right than Hemingway.)

So, this made me re-think why I like *The Sun Also Rises* so much that I have read it at least three times. (And I do not often re-read books.) And the reasons I came up with point to why literature is important, especially to a marketer. They are:

- *The tone of the book*: Hemingway perfectly captures the emotional tone of a particular time, place and group of people. No book better sums up the Lost Generation. (I like the Lost Generation because it produced the greatest art of the 20th Century, as great losses tend to do. This is the same reason why there are so many good Southern writers, the South having suffered a tremendous loss in the Civil War and its aftermath.)

- *The point of view*: All Hemingway books see the world through the lens of a stoic, brutally honest man who is committed to engaging with the world — not because he gets any satisfaction from engaging, but simply because it is what honorable men do. I like this point of view.

- *Deft use of symbols:* Hemingway cut something like 40,000 words from *The Sun Also Rises* in an attempt to capture everything about a particular time and place — all the emotional, spiritual and psychological aspects — in the fewest possible words. Physicists consider the simplest explanation to be the most elegant. The same applies to art.

Literature is important to the marketer because it teaches her how to use symbols skillfully to set a tone and present a believable point of view that will connect with her target audience. It is not important because it teaches us moral or life lessons — the pages of most works of literature are peopled with scalawags and scamps — but because it teaches us how to use words in ways that communicate more than the sum of their face value. It teaches us how to skillfully manipulate symbols to generate an emotional response, rather than a strictly rational one. (And a strictly rational response may not always be the right or healthy choice. The best choices blend rational and emotional information.)

I think this goes a long way toward explaining why my "rational" book club did not like Hemingway. The content of *The Sun Also Rises* is almost entirely emotional, and not even healthy emotions. There are no life lessons to learn from this book. You are not a better person for having read it. You may be a more aware person, but not necessarily a better one.

Since most buying decisions are based on satisfying an emotion that we cover in patina of reason, knowing how to generate an emotional response with marks on a page is a very useful skill for the marketer.

And that is why literature matters.

Show, Don't Tell

In *A Swim In A Pond In The Rain*, award-winning novelist and professor George Saunders presents a master's course in literary interpretation through analysis of seven short stories by renowned Russian authors.

Reading Saunders' exegesis of Anton Chekhov's *Gooseberries* was the first time I understood how literature can communicate differently, certainly more effectively and more deeply, than reportage, essays or other logically oriented, objective writing. I learned that the most important message in a story emerges from actions that tell a subconscious narrative: a narrative that can be different than, even opposed to, what the words say, or what words alone can say.

> *Communication via action delivers a much more powerful,*
> *more rounded, more emotional, even spiritual message*
> *than words alone can do.*

In other words, effective messages often emerge from a "show, don't tell" approach.

For example, in *Gooseberries* two men come upon a dacha (a cottage) in the woods. They are tired of walking in the rain and look forward to getting out of it and getting some bread and vodka in their bellies. The first thing one of the men does when he gets there is take a swim in the pool while the other waits in the house, demonstrating, Saunders says, that the swimmer is totally self-absorbed, ignoring his friend until it is convenient, as the action in the rest of the story supports.

This communication via action — instead of, even contra to the surface narrative — delivers a much more powerful, more rounded, more emotional, even spiritual message than words alone could have done. Why not employ this approach in marketing?

Well, you might say, it's already being done. Product demonstration is the oldest kind of TV spot. Yes, but setting up a scene about a product with no product reference, no words — even just showing the product doing what it does while a different script is playing on the surface — has never been done.

And I'm not talking about movie product placements either, which usually do not advance the plot and are little more than scenery. Product placements help solidify the ubiquity of an established brand, but they don't motivate someone, they don't reveal a desire to buy at an unconscious/conscious level — that is, at the border of the unconscious, where consciousness begins working, where it is able to perceive hints, ghosts and whisps from the unconscious. This is a powerful, primal connection to a brand.

How might one market at this border to the underworld? By creating and starring in a story, of course — a sequence of actions that communicates more than the actual narrative.

I submit that Elon Musk is a prime example of selling a story to advance a business. The story, of course, is his life, which is theatre. He fired his PR department yet gets more coverage — most of it positive — than any other CEO I can think of. He communicates verbally pretty frequently, of course, but often little more than "Watch this!" And visuals are always part of the message — from photos in tweets to otherworldly pickup trucks in the room. Most photos you see of Musk are with something he created or the place where he created it and ran it. And running it is definitely part of the story. This is not a startup cowboy who can't build things.

His myth (and his companies' myth) is that of the indomitable force. Something that exists because it chooses, because it creates its own reality and shares it with us. Musk simply acts — like building an entire industry on nothing but intelligence and unrelenting work. And his story — which is not about his products, but about his existence — transfers to his products, which are viewed as almost mythically smart, effective and even inspiring. His story is about setting and achieving ever more difficult conquests. It's the American success story writ large.

Another great mythical marketing story — and another example of the founder's commitment to action and honesty — is Southwest Airlines. The atmosphere on a Southwest flight is what it was probably like to be in the same room with co-founder Herb Kelleher — irreverent, a bit sarcastic, but fundamentally kind and considerate Herb lived large — smoking, drinking, telling jokes — but the planes flew on time, and Southwest did honest, common-sense things that other airlines were afraid of trying, like open seating, providing peanuts instead of meals, flying into secondary airports. And Southwest acts without regard for convention, like encouraging stewardesses and stewards to do stand-up acts during the mandatory safety speech. Or frankly, just telling the unalloyed truth, like the Southwest steward I flew with in 2020 who peppered his pre-flight monologues with riffs on how awful flying is in the age of COVID.

And that is Southwest's story — the airline that tells the truth, no matter what. The no-BS airline.

Sure, you say, but you've simply described brands. Perhaps, but I guess I see a brand as strictly or predominantly a verbal and visual creation, messages and images that are processed in the frontal cortex and are clearly and frequently communicated via standard symbols of headlines, copy and scripts. A story is the myth of how the company acts over time and what it acts on and the narrative that traces — and such information resides in an older, more primitive part of the brain, home of instinct and reflex.

Some products don't have a narrative because the people behind them don't have a path, just motion. Does your company have a story or just a history? Do you need to find a path or at least a clear destination or motivation? My advice: don't read more business books to find what you are looking for. Read literature.

- Originally appeared in Forbes

The Color of Money

Color choices for marketing materials are often the most subjective decisions clients make. We have learned to simply ask what clients like and go with it, because preferred colors are an entirely emotional matter.

I'm the same way. I have a personal attraction to yellow – all shades of it, but particularly ochre, which I associate with Robert Motherwell and Mark Rothko, two of my favorite painters, as well as with ancient walls in Italy. And, of course, I am especially partial to PMS 123, the Bradford Group's corporate color.

There is a science to color.

What if we led with our head instead of our heart? Might we create more effective brochures, booklets, posters, annual reports, flyers, mailer, websites and infographics?

Maybe. There is a science to color, which *American Demographics* did an excellent job of explaining many years ago in its Feb. 2002 issue. Below is their skinny on color choices. It might come in handy for your next marketing project.

Red

- Attributes: exciting, daring, dynamic, sexy, intense, impulsive, active, aggressive, passionate
- Associated with: blood, fire, competition, heat, emotion, optimism, violence, communism
- Effect: arousal, stimulation, increases heart and respiratory rate
- Preferred by: achievers, high-powered, active women, most economically stable, most secure

Orange

- Attributes: in your face, vibrant, warm
- Associated with: extroversion, adventure, celebration

- Effect: stimulating but less than red, triggers alert
- Preferred by: Influentials, adolescents, second least favorite color overall

Yellow

- Attributes: the warmest color, cheerful, happy
- Associated with: sunshine, creativity, imagination, optimism, futuristic, spirituality, newness, low prices
- Effect: warming, cheering
- Preferred by: the first color kids reach for, but the least preferred color overall

Green

- Attributes: fresh, clean, restful
- Associated with: ecology, nature, balance, envy, fertility, spring
- Effect: stabilizing, nurturing, healing, revitalizing
- Preferred by: Influentials, opinion leaders, trendsetters, second most favorite color overall

Blue

- Attributes: calm, tranquil, holy
- Associated with: constancy, dependability, water, sky, holiness, protection, purity, peace, trust, loyalty, patience, hope, perseverance
- Effect: calming, cleansing, cooling
- Preferred by: No. 1 favorite color in America, No. 1 for casual clothes, No. 2 for business clothes

Purple

- Attributes: exciting, mysterious, complex, intriguing
- Associated with: passion, spirituality, art, creativity, wit, sensitivity, vanity, moodiness, royalty, superiority, homosexuality, richness
- Effect: inspiring, thought-provoking, polarizing

- Preferred by: No. 3 favorite color overall, popular among 18-29-year-olds, artists, more androgynous than other colors, loved or hated more than any other color

Brown

- Attributes: comfortable, reliable, steady, simple
- Associated with: earth, substance, stability, harmony, hearth, home, neutrality
- Effect: comforting, soothing
- Preferred by: practical people, down-to-earth people, Midwesterners, non-coastals

Black

- Attributes: mysterious, elegant, sophisticated, worldly, sexy, powerful
- Associated with: sophistication, simplicity, death and mourning, bad luck, night, power, evil
- Effect: empowering
- Preferred by: intellectuals, rebels, fashion industry, increasingly broad in appeal

White

- Attributes: clean, fresh, pure, modern, neat
- Associated with: purity, sterility, calm, brides
- Effect: eyestrain, headaches, attention-getting
- Preferred by: intellectuals, modern types, limited appeal overall

Management

I am not a natural manager. Running a business is much more mysterious to me than practicing public relations and marketing. The lessons communicated in the following pages were hard-won over 20 years of starting, running and selling a business. There's nothing academic here.

The greatest lesson I learned – and it took a long time – is that the most important thing any business does is build and motivate an outstanding team of people. In the following pages, I share my experiences in learning this lesson, as well as lessons from the great and mighty on how to lead people.

How To Create a Great Company Culture

Do you want a great company culture that attracts and retains outstanding people? That motivates people to do their best and prevents burnout? That puts joy back into work?

Every company has a culture, of course. It's just that most are accidental. If you're an especially charismatic leader your company might naturally have a wonderful culture. But accidental cultures are usually less than wonderful.

> *Every company has a culture, of course.*
> *It's just that most are accidental.*

In my experience, building a strong culture is a matter of two things: 1) agreeing on and adhering to specific values and 2) establishing a routine of actions that are guided by those values.

For example, at our firm, we live by three values:

1) *Hire smart people:* Learning is essential to growth, and everybody here wants to grow. Smart people are also more effective than people of average intelligence, so we also do a better job for our clients.

2) *Be proactive:* We should see what needs to be done and do it, not wait for a client to tell us what to do.

3) *Generate measurable results:* Clients pay us to make things happen, not just talk about making things happen.

We arrived at these values by coming together as a whole company and having an honest conversation about what really matters to us and to our clients. You'll notice that our values are not particularly highfalutin'— like you find in the annual reports of big corporations — because they are honest and actionable. They are ideas that we really rely on to run our business, not just words on a wall meant to impress visitors, but that no one in the company can remember.

We live our values through a series of regular activities:

- *Quarterly planning sessions:* During which we evaluate how well the company is living out its values, celebrate our successes and make plans to improve in the next quarter. And our plans include specific, measurable outcomes, so they drive results.

- *Fortnightly progress meetings:* Every member of our company meets every two weeks with his or her superior to evaluate how well they are progressing toward their goals and, if corrective action is needed, to figure out what the employee and the company need to do to get back on track. Though these meetings are goal-directed, they also provide a regular opportunity for staff members to talk about how things are going and how they feel — so they feel listened to, and so management gets an early warning of trouble brewing.

- *Daily huddles:* Every morning we all gather for a quick 5-minute stand-up meeting during which we report on how we are progressing on meeting our goals, talk about what is on our plate that day, ask for help if we need it and declare the "One Thing" we will accomplish that day no matter what. It's amazing how much such a simple daily meeting can do to create a sense of teamwork.

- *Celebrate everyday successes:* Every time someone does something worth celebrating, everyone is encouraged to write it down on a slip of paper, noting which of our three values this success evinces, and put it up on our "kudos board." Then, once a quarter, we take down all the "kudos" and recognize the people who gave and received the most. Winners get a chance to spin the "wheel of bliss" and win a prize, ranging from an Amazon gift card to a free day off with pay.

- *Knock off early on Fridays and share a beer together:* At 4:30 every Friday afternoon, we stop working and gather in the office kitchen to share a beer or a glass of wine together. It's a pleasant way to de-stress at end the week and helps to create bonds that sustain us through tough times.

All these actions have one thing in common: they are about trusting people — trusting that everyone wants what is best for the company, that they will bring their best to job and that we will be honest with each other about what we want and what we need to deliver the best results to our clients. It's about treating people like the smart adults they are, because when you come down to it, that's what a great culture is: an environment where people are treated with respect, expectations are clear, successes are celebrated and problems are dealt with, not wished away.

- Originally appeared in Forbes

How To Create Vision and Mission Statements That Aren't a Joke

What is the purpose of your organization?

Defining your company's vision and mission is crucial to effectively presenting your brand, as well as assuring your company operates effectively. A company's vision and mission keep it on task and drive it forward.

Vision statements are about looking ahead. They state where you want to *go*. Mission statements are about what you *do*. They outline the actions and results needed to achieve your vision.

> *Vision and mission statements can play a seminal role in defining the overall aim and direction of the company, if you take them seriously and invest the time required.*

Vision and mission statements should be:

- *Aspirational,* in that they are about what you want to accomplish, the difference you want to make.

- *Inspirational,* because they are the emotional foundation that supports your day-to-day work. (The root of the word "inspiration" relates to breathing life into things.)

- *Motivational,* by providing a basis and reason for your work.

For example, Amazon's vision statement is "To be Earth's most customer-centric company, where customers can find and discover anything they might want to buy online." It clearly states the company's desired future.

For an effective mission statement, consider Disney's: "The mission of The Walt Disney Company is to be one of the world's leading producers and providers of entertainment and information. Using our portfolio of brands to differentiate our content, services and consumer products, we seek to develop the most creative, innovative and profitable entertainment experiences and related products in the world." It explains exactly how they are going to attain their vision of making people happy.

So how do you go about writing a vision and mission statement?

Step 1. Start with your company's "Why"

Why was the company started? Why in your particular industry? Why do you want to succeed? Once you know why you do what you do, it'll be easier to put your vision and mission into words.

Step 2. Answer the big questions

Before you start formulating your statements, take the "Why" you came up with and flesh it out with answers to these questions.

For your vision statement:

- What's the purpose of your organization?

- How does your organization make the world a better place?

- What problems does your organization solve?

- What's your ultimate aim for the organization?

For your mission statement:

- What do you do?

- Who benefits from these actions?

- What differentiates you from competitors?

Step 3. Start formulating your message

Narrow down your answers to the above questions to the two to four main benefits your company provides, and then think about where you want those benefits to lead the company, making sure to incorporate the company's values and goals in this thought process. THEN, you can finally roll it all into those two lovely statements that define your brand.

For example, when we worked with a non-profit staffing firm to develop their brand, they were very clear about *why* the organization was founded: To reduce homelessness through sustainable employment.

From that, they formulated the company's vision statement: "To be the go-to employment services for families experiencing homelessness."

Then we dug into the benefits the company provides that set it apart from other staffing agencies, and broke them down into benefits to employers and benefits to homeless families.

The main benefit to employers is contained in the organization's name, Staff360 — its "360" approach to providing quality job candidates. Because Staff360 is part of a homeless shelter for families, job candidates have access to the shelter's case management services, which helps them deal with the "life" issues that often plague low skill workers, such as housing, family dynamics and budgeting. This means employers get workers who are less likely to be distracted by problems in their life and more likely to be motivated to do an excellent job.

The main benefit to job candidates is getting access to jobs along with the support they need to escape the trap of homelessness, thanks to Staff360's holistic commitment to helping their clients.

From this flowed their mission statement: "Use the holistic Staff360 approach to help people achieve a satisfying career and help companies find quality employees."

Try to be as specific as possible when creating your mission statement so that you have a clear guide toward your vision. It is the framework for your company's roadmap, so you want to be able to create direct steps to follow that will lead to your company's goals.

While vision and mission statements can seem a little hokey, they can play a seminal role in defining the overall aim and direction of the company, if you take them seriously and invest the time required.

- Originally appeared in Forbes

How To Hire Smart People

"Hire Smart People" is the first of our PR firm's three core values. We have to use our heads a lot, so we want to make sure the heads have big brains in them.

Why? Because skills can be acquired, knowledge can be learned, experience can be had, but intelligence is pretty much a fixed commodity, at least after someone is about 20 years old. Since it's unlikely we're going to grow anyone's IQ here, we need to start with high IQs to ensure everyone has the capacity to learn a lot quickly.

> *It is quite unlikely that we're going to grow anyone's IQ here, so we need to start with a high IQs to ensure everyone has the capacity to learn a lot quickly.*

I've hired many people in my career, and hiring smart people is not easy. More than once, I've found that the person who amazed me during a job interview dismays me when he starts working. Anyone who hires people has had this experience, but I tired of having it, so we devised a system for identifying and hiring the smart people who make our firm hum.

First, we care about Grade Point Averages, even if a potential employee has been out of college for years. This goes against conventional wisdom, or at least conventional thinking. *USA Today* says GPAs don't matter in the workplace. Google's senior VP of HR says that "GPAs are worthless as a criteria for hiring." Search for "does GPA matter?" You'll find page after page of soothing bromides for C students. Even *PR Daily* writes about "The 9 things that matter more to employers than grades."

Are we wrong? Do we need to look beyond mediocre academic performance to find the real superstar within? Well, I do not have the time nor inclination to open 1,000 clams on the chance of finding one pearl. There are too many pearls in clear sight — the smart, hard-working people who earned GPAs of 3.5 (B+) or better.

Other discriminating employers agree. According to *Forbes*, such well-run companies as Kellogg, Procter & Gamble, Bank of America and Ernst & Young won't look at candidates with a GPA below 3.0 – and many won't go below 3.5, which is the threshold at our firm.

We care about GPA because is it a reasonably accurate indicator of traits we care about, which includes intelligence, work ethic, discipline and organizational ability. It is terribly hard to earn good grades without these things, and we've found that the academically gifted people we hire have these things in abundance – which is why more than half of our staff graduated *magna* or *summa cum laude*. (I'm not among them, by the way. I believe in hiring people who are smarter than I am. My 3.5 GPA barely squeaks by our threshold.)

Of course, through some combination of a school's lax academic standards and a student's cunning, it is possible for someone to graduate college with a GPA that indicates they are more capable than they really are, which is why we also test to assure that what is in peoples' heads matches up with what is on their resumes.

Because writing is central to our profession, we begin with a writing test and a proofreading test, which we send to everyone who applies for a job. We don't look at anything else – resume, cover letter, references or GPA – before we review the results of these tests. If the results are superb, then we look at the other supporting information. (*See chapter "How To Hire Great Writers" for more about writing tests.*)

If the writing and proofing tests are done well and everything else looks great – strong GPA, pertinent experience, evidence of leadership and initiative – we invite the candidate to a personal interview. First, our COO and I interview the candidate for about an hour, then we ask the entire team to interview their potential new team member. This second interview is important for several reasons: 1) We get to see how the candidate does in a group situation. 2) We get a different perspective on the candidate's skills. And 3) we get to see if the chemistry is right, that is, if this person would work well with the rest of the team. We also give the candidate a personality test to further probe whether they are the right fit for our team.

If all goes well, there is one final test: an aptitude test that measures general intelligence. The 60-minute timed test measures the candidate's agility in verbal, mathematical and spatial reasoning. Though it is not technically an IQ test, which might be a bit creepy, it does show where one ranks in the general population per mental acuity. As a rule, we hire only people in the top two quintiles of general intelligence.

So, that is our system for finding smart people:

1) *Writing test*: to gauge facility with the language — not just grammar and syntax, but also general creativity and ability to communicate clearly, logically and succinctly.

2) *Proofreading test*: for knowledge of grammar, spelling, punctuation and, most importantly, attention to detail.

3) *GPA*: at least 3.5, preferably graduated with honors.

4) *Two intensive in-person interviews*: which focus on the candidate telling us exactly how they did the things listed on their resume, why they want to work for our company — and a lot of other topics we'll not divulge.

5) *Intelligence test*: to make sure they have the intellectual horsepower needed to think clearly, deeply and quickly.

6) *Personality test*: to make sure they fit with the team.

And then, of course, we call references. If they are not absolutely glowing, we do not make the hire. We expect good references — who is going to list someone who will give them a bad reference? A glowing reference confirms what all our testing and interviewing told us; anything less is a red flag.

It is hard work finding smart people, but it is absolutely essential. Our only product is what comes out of our heads, so the heads producing it must be the very best. And they are.

How To Write an Employee Manual People Will Actually Read

When I turned to our company's employee manual for information to fill out an award nomination, I was surprised by how good it is.

Our manual is different than most in that it sprang up from within the company, rather than handed down from on high. The CEO (me) had no hand in creating it. (Which explains my surprise at what I found). It is largely the creation of our COO, who is keeper of our company culture, with contributions from other team members.

> *It honestly and clearly says who we are,*
> *what kind of people are likely to succeed here*
> *and how you can be one of them.*

This communal method of creating our handbook may account for its unique nature — being more about who we are and why we exisit than about rules to follow.

Fully alive, rooted in values

Our company's employee handbook begins with an immersion into our company as it is right now by providing links to all our social media feeds as well as a link to our blog, to which everyone in the company contributes an average of one post per month. These links on Page One of the manual assure that this document won't become a moribund tome of old ideas and old ways — and it keeps us honest, because it is easy to compare who we are with who the handbook says we are.

Following right behind these links — on the same page — is a listing of our three core values and our core purpose. This juxtaposition of the immediate and the timeless communicates that our commitment to staying current is grounded in an unwavering dedication to what we stand for.

Getting to know us

Next is a section of short biographies of every member of the Bradford Group that combine the personal and the professional. Professionally, the bio gives a brief history of the staff member's career, an overview of what he or she does at the agency — and what he or she values, so you get a sense of who the person is, not just what they do. For example, my bio says I "place a high value on our writing abilities and organized creativity." On the personal side, you learn the name of my wife, and how many children and dogs we have. You'll also learn that "He can be heard singing and whistling when he is strolling down the hall or in his office."

And you also get a glimpse into each staff member's personality through the inclusion of a DiSC diagram in the bio, that is, a diagram that shows the percentage of Dominance, Influence, Steadiness and Conscientious in his or her personality. (Everyone is also trained in how to understand DiSC scores to foster better communication throughout the company.)

Buddy up to meet expectations

The next section explains the Bradford Buddy System, whereby new hires are partnered with a seasoned staff member to show them the ropes, and "to have a designated resource for discussing things and/or asking questions that may seem uncomfortable to address in front of a superior or the whole group."

Then we clearly lay out what is expected of anyone who becomes a member of our team. Basically, this describes the attitude that successful team members demonstrate, more so than the specific expectations of your job. For example, you are expected to "Set and meet high standards in all we do," "Be very proactive," "Use 'we' more than 'I'" and "Understand that your areas of responsibility may change and expand."

Nuts and bolts

This high level information is followed by very specific, no-nonsense information about how we work — such as the regular meetings we have and your role in these meetings, the fun things we regularly do and how you can participate, what stuff in the frig you can consume and what is strictly for clients, when to empty the dishwasher (whenever it needs it), how our slightly weird thermostats work, and, grammar-wise, to never use an Oxford comma and don't double-space after a sentence, to a name a few of our rules of the road.

How to be great

There is, of course, also information about company policies and perks, but instead of the usual legalistic pablum found in the typical employee handbook, most of the rest of the book is about how to excel at being a member of our firm. Topics include how to run a client meeting (complete with a sample agenda), how to write a blog, how to take a photograph that a news outlet will use, how to pitch a news story, how to write well (with links to examples), what clients expect and how to proactively exceed their expectations.

It is truly a remarkable document — something that new hires (and 20-year-veterans, like me) will want to read, because it honestly and clearly says who we are, what kind of people are likely to succeed here and how you can be one of them. I'm proud to be part of a company that knows itself well enough to lay all of it out over 47 well-written pages and is confident enough to share it with everyone on the team.

- Originally appeared in Forbes

How To Design an Office That Makes You More Productive

Creative industries are often at the forefront of office design. Think *Mad Men*-esque advertising agencies in the 1950s, with rooms designed specifically for imbibing cocktails with prospective clients. Or the Silicon Valley offices of the 21st Century, complete with volleyball courts and employees sitting on beanbags sporting laptops and ear buds.

Despite such design innovations, the open floor plan used in many office spaces to spur creativity may, in fact, be hampering employees' creative abilities. Research shows that creativity is cultivated in the workplace through a combination of structure and fluidity.

> *Office design that enhances creativity and encourages*
> *productivity blends areas of collaboration*
> *and open exchange with areas of quiet.*

From choosing the right decorative colors to having designated spaces of quiet, the recipe for maximum creativity is a blend of innovative and tried-and-true office design principles, and that balance looks differently than the open-office trend that's become a symbol of progressiveness.

A room of one's own

Though open office layout can give the impression of an innovative, go-with-the-flow company, organizational psychologist Matthew Davis found that open layout offices led to decreased levels of concentration and increased levels of stress — far more so than in work settings that mix offices and open space.

The feeling of psychological privacy that comes with individual offices also enhances job performance. Not to mention what an open office layout does to noise levels. Studies have also shown that even a small amount of background noise increases mental workload, which further contributes to employee stress and lowered productivity.

The most effective office design for enhancing creativity and encouraging productivity blends areas of collaboration with areas of quiet where private, focused work can occur.

Creating designated spaces within the office doesn't have to be an eye sore. The designer who designed the space for our PR firm said she doesn't just design the environment; she designs experience and behavior. Office design should reflect the different work modes people experience every day. In addition to offering spaces where people can close the door and put their heads down to work, an office should allow for spontaneous work to happen.

The modern break room is an example. No longer are they places behind closed doors. Instead, they take up the spaces that might have gone to the head honcho a decade ago, where there's an abundance of natural light and a killer view of the city skyline (like at our offices). The break rooms of today tend to have a bistro or café feel to them — a place that encourages people to talk and collaborate. And more connected employees mean happier, more creative employees.

Let there be light

In the same way that plants need the sun, so too is creativity dependent on natural light. Integrating sunlight into office design — and making sure it shines on all employees — is vital to creating the environments where creative ideas grow.

Studies prove that natural light has mood-enhancing effects that encourage creativity. Janetta Mitchell McCoy, an interior design professor at Washington State University (WSU), found that when high school students designed collages in environments with elevated levels of natural light, the results were more innovative.

Increased levels of natural light also encourage the appearance of office plants, which have been proven to lower workplace stress and increase productivity. Another study out of WSU found that when plants were added to the lab, subjects reacted 12% more quickly on computer tasks and had lower blood pressures. Thinking of office space as a greenhouse of creativity should be a guiding principle for developing spaces conducive to encouraging creative thought.

Organic shapes

Have you ever thought that modern design, complete with its over-abundance of white and 90-degree angles, looked interesting to the eye but felt so sterile you'd rather be operated on than have a meaningful conversation? There's a scientific reason for that. A study led by Oshin Vartanian of the University of Toronto found that participants judged curvilinear spaces as more beautiful than rectilinear ones and that their decisions were largely driven by feelings of pleasantness.

The pleasantness or feelings of ease derived from curved spaces are primal reactions. Geologist Jay Appelton's "habitat theory" postulated that the perception of an environment as favorable or unfavorable to survival is a primary determinant for finding a landscape aesthetically pleasing. A sterile or unnatural space, which is often the result of modern design trends, may be alerting our brains to conditions unsuitable for flourishing.

Round edges and circular design don't just put creative people subconsciously at ease and free up their minds to innovate. Curved edges also inspire spontaneous conversation, which can be a catalyst of creative thought. The U.S. Census Bureau kept this in mind when designing their new headquarters. Instead of lining up desks lengthwise, as was the case in their previous offices, the architects elected for curved edges in places with possible pedestrian traffic. A less rigid design allows for more organic movement among employees, encouraging run-ins that may not have happened otherwise.

Rorschach test

"How does that make you feel?" is a legitimate question to ask outside of the therapist's office. It should be asked when designing an office space because color, and even the smallest decorative objects, are factors in spurring creative thinking. Psychologist Robert Epstein, a visiting scholar at the University of California, San Diego, says that surrounding people with unusual objects helps encourage out-of-the-ordinary thoughts. Color selection is often seen as a subjective choice, but it turns out that colors and certain shapes elicit universal reactions from people. *(See "The Color of Money" chapter.)*

Finally, beyond the psychological benefits to creativity and productivity, these design principles are also tools for generating new business and attracting high-quality talent. Creating an environment where it's clear that employees are serious about their work, but still open to collaboration, signals to potential clients and potential employees that your company thinks in innovative ways and generates results.

- Originally appeared in Fast Company

How To Successfully Merge Companies

On March 1, 2020, exactly 20 years after the day it was founded, my PR firm, the Bradford Group, merged with 30-year-old Dalton Agency, becoming the Nashville office of a three-city agency with a staff of 100.

It was a big win for everyone — more resources across more disciplines for our clients, more opportunities for our employees, better technology and more opportunities to sell our services to a broadened base of prospects. Not only did clients and employees well-receive the news of this merger, but it also boosted our reputation in the local business community.

If you are prepared, are transparent with your employees and keep them in the loop, you will find merging your firm with another to be one of the best business decisions of your life.

Of course, it could have been a disaster. Here are some lessons we learned about how to do a merger right:

Culture is key

Right up front, make sure the cultures of the two organizations mesh well. It begins at the top: If the two CEOs get along, the chances are good that their organizations will also, as the culture of most companies primarily manifests the CEO's personality. But it's not always a sure thing. So, quickly after the deal is signed, it's vital that the CEO of the company with which yours merged come to your place for a Q&A with your employees. They need to get to know him and trust him. Transparency is important from Day One.

Take it slow, but don't procrastinate

People need time to digest a big announcement like a merger, so don't start moving desks around the first day. Give it a little time to sink in. But don't wait too long to start taking concrete action to blend the two organizations into one, because you run the danger of employees thinking nothing will change, which can cause anxiety when (not if) things do change.

Get everyone involved in the integration

One of the best things we did was set up about a dozen integration teams — and put just about every employee in the two formerly separate companies on one of the teams. There were teams to study integrating tech systems, to integrate messaging, to integrate and coordinate perks and benefits, and many more. Creating these teams assured that this important work of creating one company out of two was accomplished, and involving everyone assured that employees felt part of this new thing we built — because they helped shape it.

Communicate, communicate, communicate

Our new firm is spread across three cities — Nashville, Atlanta and Jacksonville. This geographic reach, combined with the fact that our merger occurred just as the COVID pandemic was beginning, presented challenges to creating a common culture. So, we over-communicated to compensate, holding a series of agency-wide and departmental meetings via video conference on a regular basis for the first six months after the merger. Some of these meetings were just fun, designed to introduce us to each other. Others were all business. But they all worked to bring us together and feel like a team.

Clear messaging

Being a PR firm, we, of course, knew the importance of clear messaging and getting the message right was the first thing we did. Then we made sure that everyone — and we mean everyone in the company — knew what our messages were, assuring that we consistently communicated the same thing across all channels, not just media channels, but family, friends, church, competitors and others. Everyone.

Don't let your clients read about it first in the newspaper

Soon after the merger has become official — and right after employees are told — reach out to your clients and let them know the good news.

The key here is to assure clients that they can expect to get everything they've always looked to you for — that nothing has changed in how you do business or in your commitment to them — but that now you have even more to offer. Informing clients is the scariest part of this entire process, but I was pleasantly surprised how drama-free it was. They were all delighted to hear the news and quickly saw the benefits.

Hit the ground running on sales

You can be sure that your competitors will attempt to tell a different story than the one you are telling, i.e., that things are sure to change for the worse at your firm after the merger, that clients will probably suffer from lack of attention, that the merger was to solve a deep problem, and so forth. The best way to fight back against this assault, in addition to getting out the news yourself and controlling the story, is to immediately ramp up your sales efforts. And you will find sales much easier than before, because the merger gave you a lot more capabilities to offer.

Carefully change the name

Dalton needed to figure out the value of what he'd purchased. Was it a brand or a person? He found it was a bit of both. The brand was partly Jeff Bradford and partly the Bradford Group. Brand-wise, of course, it would have been better if it was simply the Bradford Group. But, by golly, we had created a happy band of PR pros. For the last seven or eight years, we had really focused on company culture, and we were well-known as one of Nashville's top PR firms.

So, there was certainly market awareness of the Bradford Group, brand equity to be had. How do you harvest it?

In our case, by operating under a dual name for a year — the Bradford Dalton Group, with the same logomark and colors as Bradford. We were selling, in effect, Bradford with Dalton resources. And it worked. Bradford Dalton was a good transitional tactic for a relational firm like ours, where we regularly meet with our clients. The conjunction of names was easy to understand and made sense.

And then, one day there was Dalton only. The Dalton Agency emerged in Nashville, our hometown, as the unified brand of a three-city agency, with me as president of the Nashville office. We handed out new business cards to all staff, changed out the big logo hanging in the lobby and the one on the exterior of our building, painted Dalton orange over Bradford yellow throughout the offices, changed our email signatures and a few other signifiers. But we did not officially announce anything. We simply began operating under an abbreviated version of the name we had used for the past year: Dalton instead of Bradford Dalton.

And it was like nothing happened. Not a rustle from any client, employee, community leader, competitor, friend or foe. The change was immediately accepted as an upgrade, thanks to a year of showing off our new capabilities as Bradford Dalton. And business went on as usual. It wasn't that our 20-year history was meaningless, but that it meant a lot more to me than it did to anybody else. Which is a lot of lessons rolled into one.

While I wish I could claim credit, I can't. It was all Jim Dalton's idea.

Another sign that merging was the right decision.

- Originally appeared in Forbes

How To Become a Growth Company

For about half of the 20 years of our PR firm's existence, we barely grew at all. However, once we changed our management paradigm we grew at double-digit rates.

And it's because the founder of our company (me) got out of the way and let other, more capable leaders run the show. It is a classic case of the skills needed to *start* a business being much different than those needed to *manage* an established business. Starting a business requires a high tolerance for risk, comfort with change, a ruthless focus on doing whatever it takes to make the business successful, the ability to ignore naysayers, sales skill, high energy and high expectations of everyone around you.

> *The founder of our company got out of the way and let other, more capable leaders run the show.*

Some of these skills and attitudes — like ruthlessness and ignoring naysayers — are counterproductive to running (versus starting) a business. Noticeably absent from this list of business starting skills is "people skills" — which, frankly, are not my forte. However, a business, especially a professional firm like ours, depends entirely on the quality of the people who do the work. And guess what? Happy people perform much better than unhappy ones. Our business became successful when we realized this and did something about it.

Get outside help

We began our transformation by retaining a business coaching firm, Petra, that helps companies decide where they want to go and helps them get there.

A Petra coach comes to our office once a quarter for an all-day planning session during which the entire company talks about what is working and what isn't working, decides what do to about it and sets specific, measurable quarterly goals for making progress.

We worked with Petra for about eight years — and it was

transformational — especially for an English and philosophy major like me, with zero business education. We broke a million dollars a year a couple of years after beginning our relationship.

Establish a routine of accountability

The entire company gathers at 8:38 every workday morning for our 15-minute Morning Huddle, during which we share what is on our calendar for the day and our progress toward meeting our individual quarterly goals. Fortnightly, everyone in the company meets with either our COO or vice president for a one-on-one accountability meeting. And, as I mentioned above, the entire company meets quarterly to review how we are doing on achieving overall company goals for revenue, profitability and efficiency — and to set goals for the next quarter. *(For more detail on our routines of accountability, see the "How To Create a Great Company Culture" chapter.)*

Identify and made best use of your differences

Perhaps the most important thing we did to transform our company was to take stock of who we are as individuals and use this information to relate to one another in more productive ways and, more importantly, to put the right people in the right seats. This process began with everyone taking the DiSC personality profile test and sharing the results with one another. This helped us learn how best to communicate with each individual and how to best work with him or her. To make sure the word got out, we taped everyone's DiSC profile to his or her office door.

Understanding our personalities also led to perhaps the biggest shift in our operations, which was getting me out of the day-to-day management of the company and handing the job over to leaders in our company who have stronger people skills. After a lifetime of work, I finally realized that building a strong team is THE MOST IMPORANT THING a business can do — and that other people are better at this than I am. I am now focused on what I do best: sales and ideas, like helping staff members develop tactics to meet client objectives. I am happy and more productive, and so is our staff. And, as the revenue growth numbers I quoted at the beginning of this article attest to, the company benefitted greatly from this approach.

- Originally appeared in Forbes

Why Companies Should Live Their Mission Statements

In the early weeks of the Great Pandemic of 2020, I noticed a unique phenomenon: CEOs were writing open letters to their employees. And not just a few, but hundreds of CEOs (or their PR firms) were penning heartfelt missives to "their team members," assuring them that "we're all in this together."

Mission statements are now marching orders,
not just decoration.

I read and analyzed about 50 of these letters from CEOs of companies ranging in size from multinational corporations to small family businesses. I found that the best letters had four key messages:

1. The company is committed to keeping people safe.

2. The CEO empathizes with what employees are going through.

3. The CEO and company are thankful for and proud of employees for how they are conducting themselves during the pandemic.

4. The company will survive.

Companies that lived the first three of these messages were likely to live the fourth. In fact, they were likely to thrive. Those that didn't were likely victims of the Great Resignation that followed the Great Pandemic — in which millions of employees, often emboldened by increased government unemployment payments, quit their jobs.

That, at least, is the prognosis from the Gallup organization, which — about 18 months into the pandemic — published the results of a nationwide survey disclosing that an astounding 48% of American workers were actively looking for a new job or were open to new opportunities. The US Department of Labor reported that millions quit their jobs.

Why did this Great Resignation happen? Well, it appears that the rigors of the pandemic revealed many employers for who they really are. Employees found that their employers did not do all they could to keep them safe, did not genuinely empathize with them and were not particularly thankful for them. In effect, the pandemic made evident what many employees already suspected: the lofty mission and value statements printed in annual reports and proudly proclaimed on websites and in office lobbies are little more than decoration. They have scant effect on how their company operates.

For many years, business schools and business consultants have preached that a business is more than a machine for making money — that it is, rather, an organization for building people, for helping them discover their passion, for getting to "why," as one particularly breathless speaker and author of business books puts it. This exercise in selling books and making CEOs feel like saviors of humanity has always felt a little false, of course. After all, businesses *do* exist to make money. But business owners didn't want to say that out loud. Certainly not in front of employees

Eventually, employees started believing what business consultants and HR departments have proclaimed for years. They came to expect the deference given to "stakeholders." They thought their employer was concerned about helping them maintain a work-life balance. They came to believe that an employer's first obligation is to help them fulfill their personal destiny.

Then the pandemic hit. And the blinders came off. Employees found out that their company was focused first on making a profit, i.e., survival. Employees became disillusioned and then disengaged. In fact, during the latter days of the pandemic, Gallup found 74 percent of American workers were "actively disengaged."

What is an employer to do? The only thing you can do, give employees what you promised: prove that you truly care about work-life balance by being more generous with flex time and paid time off; show that you empathize with the difficult life of working parents by allowing employees to continue working from home; demonstrate how thankful you are for employees' contributions by paying them a higher wage.

This kind of care and consideration does not come cheap, of course. Your bottom line will suffer. Your customers will have to pay more. You'll have to take less — not just less money, but less autonomy in how you run your business. However, your employees are only expecting what you have been promising for years: a kinder, gentler, more giving workplace. Mission statements are now marching orders, not just decoration.

Lessons From the CEO of America's Fastest Growing Gun Company

Daniel Defense was the fastest growing gun manufacturer in the world when I met its CEO, Marty Daniel, a few years ago during a retreat for a business group. For practically the entire day we sat in the boardroom at Daniel Defense and asked Marty how he built such a successful company. It was like condensing an MBA into five hours.

Here is some of what we learned:

Hire people who already know what do to

"The biggest step your business can make is moving from hiring talent and teaching them what to do to being able to hire people that already know what to do," Marty said.

> *You don't hire people just because you can't do it all yourself. You hire people to build a team that is greater than yourself.*

Now, this doesn't mean you don't hire some entry-level people and train them up in the way you do things. That is important, too. But if you want to grow, you must hire people who have already done, and done well, what you need to get done — because having these kinds of people on your team will allow you to move beyond thinking about solving today's problems to identifying and taking advantage of tomorrow's opportunities.

Of course, these kinds of people are not cheap. Which leads us to Marty's second maxim:

Don't be afraid to pay people more than you make

Marty said it was only recently that he, the CEO, became the highest paid person in his company. When he was building his company, he had to pay people more than he made to attract and retain the best talent.

Why would a CEO pay someone more that he makes? Because that expensive person can do important things better than the CEO and therefore brings more value to the company — at least for the short-term. Over the long term, a CEO should build a company that is successful enough to pay him commiserate with the risk he assumed in starting and maintaining the company. And you build this kind of company by building an effective team.

The most important thing a CEO does is build a great management team

You hire expensive people who are smarter and more experienced than you to build a great management team — which is the foundation of a great company.

Marty realized what many entrepreneurs can't get their heads around: You don't hire people just because you can't do it all yourself. You hire people to build a team that is greater than yourself. That's what a great company is — a group of people with different, complementary skills, all the best at what they do, who focus on accomplishing something that none of them could do alone, no matter how much 'help' they hired.

Don't let them see you sweat

In fact, Marty said "pucker," not "sweat," as in, "When a CEO is in the middle of a storm, project calm to your employees: Remember, they can't see your butt pucker."

The idea is to lead through tough times, not moan about them, not "share your feelings" nor project anything other than strength, confidence and perseverance. Employees want to feel that the CEO is in charge and is not afraid to make tough decisions or face unpleasant facts and has a plan for success. "Employees don't want to think that you're oblivious to a problem, of course. That's not leadership. The message needs to be that we're not doing well right now, but we know what we are doing and will be fine," Marty said.

The reality is that everything is not always cut-and-dried. You can't control everything and plans sometimes go awry. You and your management team will need to deal with things, not just hope they go away.

All of this can naturally lead to a little clinching of your posterior. But nobody has to know but you.

Find a mentor who runs a business 10-50 times as big as yours

Do this for the obvious reason of learning from someone who has dealt with issues you've not yet dealt with — but will. But it's also to put your problems in perspective. When the CEO of a $3 billion public company talks about missing his quarterly earnings projections by $10 million, or the challenge of opening a facility in Europe, or a multi-million-unit recall, well, your problems don't seem so huge after all.

Build a team spirit of winning and losing together

Successful teams are more concerned with letting down the team than in letting down the coach, and they need to know that the team is behind them when they fail.

"The guy who drops the ball in the end zone knows he screwed up. The coach doesn't need to point this out to him. He also needs to know that the team is there to pick him up, just as they are there to lift him up when he scores," Marty said. "When you get to this point, you've got a winning team."

Lessons From Ulysses S. Grant

I enjoyed reading *Grant*, a massive biography of the Civil War general and two-term president written by Ron Chernow. In addition to learning about the life and times of Ulysses S. Grant, I also picked up some business and life lessons, which I'll share in this chapter.

Tactics beat strategy

Grant was a successful general in the Civil War because he focused on making things happen, not waiting for a grand strategy to materialize, like other Union generals. In business, I've noticed that the people who talk mostly about strategy and overarching themes actually don't get much done. You're more likely to reach your goal if you do things, not just plan them.

> *I've noticed that people who talk mostly about strategy and overarching themes actually don't get much done.*

Adapt, adapt, adapt

A focus on tactics over strategy does not mean you shouldn't have a plan, of course, and your plan should include alternative actions if things don't turn out like you planned. Things rarely go as planned on the battlefield, and Grant always had a back-up plan to rely on when the situation changed. He was able to quickly adapt his tactics to deal with reality.

Keep moving, even if you're not making progress

At the Battle of Vicksburg, a turning point in the war, Grant was stymied at first, as the city was well-fortified and geographically situated such that it was difficult to attack without Union forces being destroyed. So, he tried lots of things, some of them wild-haired, like digging a channel to bypass an oxbow in the Mississippi River. In the end, none of these ideas worked, but it kept his men busy, so they stayed sharp while Grant and his generals planned and executed a more traditional approach that did succeed.

Don't let others define who you are

Grant was pretty much a dismal failure until the Civil War gave him the chance, at the mid-point of his life, to use his natural talents as a military genius and leader. Before that, his father wanted him to take over his business, so Grant tried running a country store for a few years. He was awful at it. He had no business being in business. He was only there because someone else tried to make him who they thought he should be.

Up close and personal is harder than the 50,000 feet view

Even though he regularly saw hundreds, even thousands of men die during a battle, Grant didn't suffer emotionally until he would come upon individual soldiers who had been wounded or killed – that's when it became real for him. It's the same in business: laying off hundreds of people is a piece of cake compared to talking with one of the people who lost their job.

Writing ability is important

Being able to think and communicate clearly is the essence of leadership. Grant was an excellent writer, and this skill not only allowed him to clearly direct the actions of battalions, but it also saved his family from penury upon his death. His autobiography, which he wrote during the final months of his life, became a national best seller and the royalties supported his family when he was gone.

Look for reasons why, not why not

Until Grant rose in the ranks and captured Lincoln's attention, Union generals spent most of their time coming up with reasons why they couldn't attack. The most famous of these "why not" generals was George McClellan, whom Lincoln relieved of duty after he failed to pursue Robert E. Lee's army following the inconclusive Union victory at the Battle of Antietam – McClellan's final failure in a long string of dilly dallying. Grant kept attacking, no matter what.

I think it is possible to learn more from Grant than from other famous men, like George Washington, for example, because Grant was a flawed hero. He had a difficult time finding his place in life, he was somewhat of an alcoholic, was often depressed and his presidency was marred by scandal. He is relatable because of his flaws.

The key takeaway here for leaders, I believe, is to never give up. Don't let a failure keep you down. If you keep moving forward, the chances are good that you will eventually succeed.

- Originally appeared in Forbes

Lessons From Churchill's First Year as Prime Minister

Because Winston Churchill's first year as leader of the British people coincided with the start of World War II and was dominated by the Blitz — Germany's unrelenting eight months and five days of bombing Britain's major cities — it was fated to be one of the worst or the best initial years in political office in the history of the world.

Churchill could have easily pleaded that accomplishing anything of value in his first year was impossible, given the global crisis in which Britain found itself. The other option was to be energized by the impossibility of the challenge and accomplish historic things that could not be achieved during "typical" times, which, of course, is what he did.

> *Get in the trenches with people*
> *but not down in the gutter with them.*

The way Churchill succeeded during his first year in office offers several valuable lessons for business leaders:

Empathy matters

Churchill often wept openly — when moved by a gesture of kindness, declaring his love of England or visiting bombed-out cities — and went out of his way to share with his fellow Brits his admiration and love for them.

Almost every time he opened his mouth, even if it was to report some new atrocity, he communicated two things: 1) that he cared deeply for the British people and 2) how proud he was of the "British character" they displayed in the face of unimaginable destruction. He did not bemoan their victimhood but celebrated their refusal to be victims — and they acted like the great people Churchill told them they were.

Lesson: Make sure employees know how proud you are to work with them. Honor their character, not just their work, and they will rise to your expectations.

Actions speak louder than words

Churchill did not just talk a good game, he lived it, regularly jumping in the car to visit bombed neighborhoods and cities, witnessing the horror firsthand with everyone, consoling and encouraging the survivors. He was mobbed by well-wishers wherever he went, though these visits were never announced, and he never deliberately drew attention to himself. People would shout blessings to "Winnie" when they saw him walking by because of what he stood for, which was the dignity he was giving them by being there.

Lesson: Get in the trenches with people but not down in the gutter with them. Show by example how to uphold dignity and grace regardless of the circumstances.

Be yourself (and don't take yourself too seriously)

The "siren suit" may be the best illustration of Churchill's honest self-confidence, his fearlessness about looking foolish, his commitment to doing what felt natural and comfortable, regardless of what others thought. The siren suit — so called because it was thrown on when the air raid sirens blared and you dove for shelter — was what we know today as a jumpsuit or onesie, a one-piece outfit covering you from ankles to neck.

In other words, an outfit in which is impossible not to look silly, especially with Churchill's rotund physique. This was his everyday wear during his first year in office. Even more ridiculous, his favourite was colored sky blue. Churchill so loved the siren suit that he gave one to King George (also sky blue) for Christmas.

Lesson: Never submit to the lure of pomposity. You are much more likely to be taken seriously if you don't take yourself too seriously.

Don't be afraid to put unpopular people in positions of power

If you value competency above happiness in your organization, you'll make people unhappy as you get a lot done. And that's OK, especially during difficult times.

Max Aitken, AKA 1st Baron Beaverbrook, a British newspaper publisher who made his first million by the time he was 30 years old, was a take-no-prisoners, get-it-done kind of guy. Churchill put Beaverbrook in charge of Britain's military aircraft industry when the country's air force was all that was protecting it from total devastation by German bombers.

Beaverbrook increased the production of Britain's warplanes to two-and-a-half times that of Germany's rate of production. He also deeply and permanently angered every British bureaucrat he dealt with. That was alright because it allowed England to survive until Churchill could convince Franklin Roosevelt to get the United States in the war.

Lesson: Everything runs smoother when people are happy, but it's easy to smoothly go out of business. Be willing to shake things up.

Focus on impressing people who can help you the most

Churchill knew Britain was doomed unless the U.S. entered the war. The German war machine was simply too powerful for England to resist forever. Therefore, a secondary motive for many of Churchill's actions was to impress upon FDR that Britain could prevail with the right partner.

No one wants to back a loser, and Churchill made sure Roosevelt knew about the British people's indomitable spirit. He also argued that helping Britain helped the United States because the U.S. was next if Britain fell.

This message — 1) we're strong and can win with your help and 2) you'll suffer if we fail — successfully convinced Roosevelt (and eventually Congress) to provide war material to Britain and, finally, after Pearl Harbor, to enter the war on Britain's side.

Lesson: Often a few people can dramatically affect the success or failure of your venture. Make sure they know about your success, and how they benefit from it.

As blogger Joseph Mattera noted, Churchill acted with courage, while his predecessor, Neville Chamberlain, acted in compromise. Churchill confronted reality, Chamberlain denied it. Churchill motivated greatness, Chamberlain sowed discouragement. Be more like Churchill and less like Chamberlain.

- Originally appeared in Forbes

The Brave New World of Boundless Work

Ask any business owner to list his top five problems and at least three of them will involve employees. The employer/employee relationship has been strained since it began. The fundamental disconnect is the difference in objectives: For the employer, it's building an organization that generates income and wealth for everyone, but considerably more for the owner. For the employee, it's getting the most money and best working conditions for your labor, while also enjoying what you are doing.

Hybrid working arrangements
hold the potential to be more effective and pleasant
than the ways of the 20th Century.

The tension in this naturally tense relationship is being stretched taut today by COVID-era cultural changes to the nature of work — leading to questions about whether employees should be required to come to the office or not, and if so, how often? Or should they have to work a specific number of hours during specific periods of the day? These are questions that, if asked a few years ago, would have marked the questioner as mad or, at least, frivolous. They are painfully pertinent questions today.

This is a paradigm shift in the nature of work. The boundaries of work are both expanding and contracting.

Expanding, because "work" today is basically thinking, which can be done anywhere, anytime — as long as it is done on-time and well. This makes the ground rules of work somewhat subjective and elastic because, who is to say, other than the worker herself, as to the work arrangement that best suits her life?

It also means that work is expanding into all areas of employees' lives — that the connection to "the office" is never really turned off, and not because the employer demands it, but because when work is always present, the employee often allows it to permeate his life.

On the other hand, the boundaries of work are contracting because the new model limits the ways in which people can effectively work together. For one, it severely limits mentoring, which occurs more during day-to-day interaction than through any kind of formal curriculum. This kind of interaction is possible virtually, but simply cannot be as intuitive, connected and effective as a real, live office environment. A lot is lost in translation. A generation of young workers may lose valuable assistance in their careers that used to be possible, even expected.

The boundaries are also contracting because the new paradigm deals a solid blow to collaboration and, by extension, creativity — since one is often the result of the other. Pulling several people into a conference room to discuss an opportunity or challenge remains superior to a virtual conference in both effectiveness and efficiency. (Though, admittedly, virtual client meetings are exponentially more efficient than physical meetings, considering the amount of time saved by cutting travel to meetings outside the office.)

Dealing with the shutdowns imposed by COVID rules quickly proved employees' long-standing assertions that business can be transacted, information can be shared, effective communication can occur just as well via a computer screen as in a meeting room. If not just as well, then certainly close enough, with no significant loss of fidelity to the message, the delivery or the receipt. And the bounds of work fell away like autumn leaves and blew away.

At the same time this was happening, due to demographics and government policy, there were many more jobs than there were people capable of doing them. So, guess who dictates the new rules of employment? Obviously, the owner of the scarce commodity: employees.

What is an employer to do? Honestly, get with it. The reality is that the virtual way of doing business is easier, faster, cheaper and more versatile than the old ways. If it is easier to meet someone virtually than physically, then why does physical proximity matter at all? Free your mind and your wallet will follow. Allow employees to work when they want, how they want, where they want — provided they get it done on-time and well. Care more about seeing results than seeing them around the office.

But, there's no need to throw out the benefits of office culture. I believe that the most effective business cultures of the future will be a hybrid of remote and office work. There are many benefits of a group of smart, dedicated and personable people working in close proximity and some of your people will want to spend most of their work time at the office for those reasons, and many of your people will probably want to spend some time at the office for the same reasons. The office of the future will probably be more landing pad and conference center than a row of rooms with names on the doors.

All of this will take a different mindset to make it work, and, no doubt, this new way of managing people and production is likely to be more work for management. But, in the short term, it is better for your business because you will attract and keep superior talent. And it is a winner in the long run because it is more *efficient* than the old way and holds the potential, with a bit of trial and error, to also be more *effective* and *pleasant* than the ways of the 20th Century.

- Originally appeared in Forbes

Want To Excel in Your Career? Go To the Office

Those with a "freak you" level of money, reputation and power tend to speak their minds without regard to consequences — because, for them, there frequently are no consequences, at least none that are negative. Because of this freedom from the laws of social and cultural gravity that pull down the rest of us, the "f.u." crowd is more likely to speak counter to what society and culture deign fashionable and desirable, even acceptable or permitted. That is, they are more likely to speak obvious, uncomfortable truths, and therefore, in my opinion, are worth listening to. (They are also more likely to say incredibly stupid things, so one must be discerning.)

> *You can't lead the charge*
> *if you're not at the battle.*

Today's leading mouthpiece for the unalloyed truth about discomforting topics is everybody's favorite billionaire, Elon Musk. In May 2022, Musk emailed to Tesla's executive staff that they should work at least 40 hours a week in the office or "they should pretend to work somewhere else."

Fellow f.u.-level rockstar Reed Hastings, co-CEO of Netflix, told the *Wall Street Journal* that remote work is "a pure negative." For one thing, he said, "debating ideas" is much harder in a remote environment. When asked in September 2020 if he had a date in mind for when his workforce would return to the office, Hastings said, "Twelve hours after a vaccine is approved."

JP Morgan Chase CEO Jamie Dimon, an f.u. silverback, told Reuters that remote work "... doesn't work for those who want to hustle. It doesn't work for spontaneous idea generation. It doesn't work for culture... it doesn't work for young people."

However, study after study has shown that people are more productive when they work from home, as well as happier and healthier. Everyone is extolling the virtues of this Brave New World of remote work, which seems to bring record-breaking levels of productivity and employee satisfaction. Why would powerful people — i.e., people who are often insensitive to cultural and societal condemnation — take such a hard line against a universally benighted concept?

Perhaps because they're right. Speaking as the owner of a business in a creative industry staffed exclusively by the knowledge workers for whom remote work was designed, I believe the negatives outweigh the positives, particularly for the young workers who are most vociferous about working remotely.

First, I agree with Dimon and Hastings — the quality of work is simply not as good when people are not collaborating in-person. Ideas are not generated at the same rate or quality. The energy level is lower because the driving "coopetition" that comes from working closely with smart co-workers is gone.

Morris A. Davis of Rutgers University business school said that working together in an office is energizing for the same reason that cities function as business centers. "Cities exist because... the crowding of employment makes everyone more productive," he said. "This idea also applies to firms: a firm puts all workers on the same floor of a building, or all in the same suite rather than spread throughout a building, for reasons of efficiency. It is easier to communicate and share ideas with office mates, which leads to more productive outcomes."

Second, I agree with Musk, whose main objection to remote work at Tesla and SpaceX was that it was a "benefit" available only to office workers. The people who build Tesla cars and SpaceX ships don't have the luxury of working from their living room couch. Allowing remote work to continue post-COVID would lead to internal descension at Tesla and SpaceX, as it would at any company with a similar two-tiered workforce — which includes the nation's economic backbone of manufacturing, which is being "reshored" to the US in recent years.

It's a matter of leadership, Musk asserts, demanding that "The more senior you are, the more visible must be your presence." You can't lead the charge if you're not at the battle.

Third, the young workers who are most enthusiastic about remote work are the most likely to suffer from this transformation, because they are missing out on mentoring and networking opportunities that primarily happen in the office. *TechTimes* noted of remote work that "The great resignation may have more to do with a lack of mentorship at work than anything else."

Though numerous studies show increases in productivity in a remote work environment, there are two problems with most of these studies: 1) They measure productivity, not effectiveness. That is, they measure completion of internally determined tasks, not whether the right tasks are being undertaken. They are measuring output, not effect. 2) Most of these studies track employees' self-reported productivity increases, a highly subjective and unreliable way to measure productivity. If you like getting up later, not commuting, working when you want to, having the comforts of home at work and all the other "work-life balance" perks of working from home, you're probably going to tell researchers that you are much more productive working at home. As the co-author of a study of 10,000 high-skilled remote workers put it, "I suspect that a high fraction of employees of all types, across the globe, value the flexibility, lack of a commute, and other aspects of work from home. This might bias survey respondents toward giving more positive answers to questions about their productivity."

If you are young person seeking to excel in your career, my advice is to ignore the academic studies extolling remote work and go to the office regularly. You are more likely to be involved in exciting projects and your work is more likely to be noticed — both of which will be a boon to your career. Of course, if you don't want to hustle, if just having a steady job is good enough, and if work-life balance (i.e., working less) is vitally important to you, then, by all means, stay home as long as you can. There has never been a better time to be you.

- Originally appeared in Forbes

Afterword

The True. The Good. The Beautiful.

Men own fields and farms and hills and trees. But none own the landscape.

Beauty is both an end in itself — the simple perception of natural forms is a delight — and a sign beyond itself. The presence of a higher, spiritual element is essential to its perfection. Beauty is the mark God sets upon virtue.

A single object is only beautiful as it suggests this universal grace. The world thus exists to the soul to satisfy the desire of beauty. Truth, and goodness, and beauty, are but different faces of the same All.

Ralph Waldo Emerson, who wrote everything I paraphrased up to this sentence, celebrated beauty as the most essential of the virtuous trinity of true, good and beautiful.

> *Truth and goodness are prerequisites for sustaining life.*
> *But beauty turns life into living.*

I agree. Truth and goodness are prerequisites for life. But beauty turns life into living.

Beauty can guide us to truth and goodness. It can also be an end in itself — fulfilling beyond words and concepts, "seeing the absolute order of things as they stand in the mind of God," as Emerson put it.

I believe such an aesthetic sensibility underlies the success of the best propagandists. To sense when things are right and when they're not; to see the adjustments, the edits, the nudges needed for excellence of effect; to spin a tale that taps the universal unconscious.

We have two fundamental scripts at our PR firm — our three values and our mission. The three values are: 1) *Hire smart people.* 2) *Be active marketing partners.* 3) *Generate measurable results.* This is how we do things. The reason we do them is in our mission: *Open the world to better ideas.* That is, our mission is about sharing the delight, the beauty of connecting to a better way through the products and services of our clients.

Beauty guides people to truth and goodness — literally "the goods," i.e., our clients' goods and services, which are good because they help people. And truth is inherent in any successful business, and not just in the sense of honest dealings, but, more importantly, in the ability to clearly see what is real and act accordingly.

And beauty is also the result — the delight of seeing customers satisfied, employees fulfilled and a company growing — producing a better, happier, more connected and caring world. That's propaganda in its original, truest and most beautiful sense: propagating better ideas to the world.

And for an English major, that's enough.

Colophon

This book was typeset in Goudy Old Style
using Microsoft Word on a
2013 model MacBook Pro laptop computer
running the macOS Catalina
operating system, version 10.15.7.

Goudy Old Style was created by Frederic W. Goudy
in 1915 on behalf of American Type Founders,
a business trust created in 1892
by the merger of 23 type foundries
that represented about 85% of all metal type
manufactured in the United States at the time.

An elegant and extremely legible font, Goudy Old Style
was chosen because of these characteristics
and because it is one of two typefaces
used by the author to create the first publication
he personally typeset and printed:
the Spring 1977 issue of *Vantage Point*,
the literary magazine of Centre College of Kentucky,
which the author co-edited and
printed on a hand-fed Chandler & Price 12 x 18 letterpress.

The cover illustration, licensed from Adobe Stock,
is a Chinese Communist propaganda poster
of unknown date and origin
depicting a Chinese Communist official dressed as Santa Claus
distributing propaganda messages to the proletariat.